THE TRADITIONAL
AGA
BOOK OF
VEGETARIAN
COOKING

THE TRADITIONAL
AGA
BOOK OF
VEGETARIAN
COOKING

Louise Walker

Absolute Press

First published in
Great Britain in 2002 by

Absolute Press
Scarborough House
29 James Street West
Bath BA1 2BT
England
Phone 44 (0) 1225 316013
Fax 44 (0) 1225 445836
E-mail info@absolutepress.co.uk
Website www.absolutepress.co.uk

Reprinted 2005

A catalogue record of this book is
available from the British Library

ISBN 1 899791 29 9

Cover and text illustrations
by Caroline Nisbett

Printed and bound
by Legoprint, Italy

CONTENTS

GENERAL INTRODUCTION

INTRODUCTION

Through my Aga demonstrations I've discovered that more and more people are becoming vegetarians or only eat limited amounts of meat and fish. This is a book written by a 'side-line' vegetarian, in other words, like many people, I eat an ever decreasing amount of meat and find vegetarian recipes very appealing.

For my cookery demonstrations at home and in Aga showrooms I always try to provide at least one vegetarian dish. Over the last three or four years I have noticed an increased demand for a vegetarian dish at Christmas as so many families have at least one vegetarian to stay and, knowing Aga owners, the vegetarian cannot be fobbed off with cheese and biscuits or something boring from the supermarket.

This book is really only one starting point for ideas for vegetarian dishes, but I hope that true vegetarians and part-time vegetarians alike will find recipes that spark the imagination and the taste buds.

Over the course of writing this book there have been a few notes on equipment, ingredients and techniques that may need longer explanation. I am the world's worst at reading introductions in cookery books, but if you can spare me a few minutes you may find some things later in the book easier to follow!

Metric/imperial conversion. This is a topic that exercises my brain a lot. Nearly every Aga owner that I have spoken to prefers to work with imperial measures even though we buy our food in metric quantities. So many of our basic recipes that we know by heart are in imperial so conversion can be difficult. Throughout this book I have given both metric and imperial measurements except where it is now only possible to buy in metric. In some cases giving a conversion can lead to silly amounts in imperial. I can't think of any recipe where weighing of ingredients has to be precise. For me one of the most difficult aspects of writing a book is having to weigh everything. Those who have been to my cookery demonstrations know that I like the phrase 'about so much...'.

Cooking with an Aga is not a precise science. I can't count the number of different Agas that I cook on each year and they all differ. Even your own Aga – however well you know it – may vary in temperature and cooking speed depending upon the wind direction. So my instructions can only be a guideline. Keep a pencil handy to mark cooking variations in your recipe book.

CONVERSION CHART

This is the metric/imperial chart that I abide by. Do keep to either metric or imperial measures throughout the whole recipe. Mixing the two can lead to all kinds of problems. Eggs used in testing have been size 3. "Tablespoon" and "teaspoon" measures have been flat unless otherwise stated.

Ingredients	Conversion
1 oz	25g
2 oz	50g
3 oz	75g
4 oz	100g
5 oz	150g
6 oz	175g
7 oz	200g
8 oz	225g
9 oz	250g
10 oz	275g
11 oz	300g
12 oz	350g
13 oz	375g
14 oz	400g
15 oz	425g
16 oz (1 lb)	450g
2 lb	1kg
1 tsp	5ml
1 tbsp	15ml
¼ pint	150ml
½ pint	300ml
¾ pint	450ml
1 pint	600ml
2 pints	1.2l
8-inch tin	20-cm tin

LOOKING AFTER YOUR AGA

Over the last few years Aga-Rayburn have brought out a few new items of cookware. I am lucky in that I can try these in the showrooms during cookery demonstrations before I buy. Utensils are expensive and so you need to know that you will get value for money. All the Aga Shops and dealer's shops should have a good range of equipment. All the items made for Aga have been tested and, if looked after, will last as long as your Aga. I have seen a set of saucepans bought with a new Aga 48 years ago and just one handle had come off in that time! Remember to dry everything well before putting away, but that is easy, wash and put straight back on the Aga to dry. Don't put aluminium trays and pans in the dishwasher, the salt will eat them!

A new Aga comes with:

> A large and small roasting tin with a grill rack inside each. These tins fit on the runners.

> A cold shelf (plain shelf) to vary the oven temperature. Keep out of the oven so that it can be effective when you need it. It is also a useful baking tray for making giant pizzas.

> Oven shelves. These are always the subject of 'help me out' at new owner demonstrations. The shelves have an anti-tilt design which is easy to use when you know what you are doing. However if you get your shelf stuck ask your service engineer or go to an Aga Shop where you can probably practice on a cold Aga. Just remember, lift the shelf up before pulling out!

> Although these are the basics that the Aga comes with, in my opinion there are three more essentials that I think new owners should buy:

> An Aga kettle. What a waste of heat it is not to use a kettle on the Aga. Do remember to give it a rinse out at least once a day

and keep it as scale-free as possible. Where I live, in Bath, we must have some of the hardest water in the country, keeping the spout of the kettle clean is a constant battle! If your kettle seems to take a long time to come to the boil give the hot plate a brush with the wire brush, just a few toast crumbs can stop the water boiling.

Gauntlets can take a little time to get used to but if you don't want burn marks up your arm they are an essential item. The Aga gauntlets can seem stiff and unwieldy when they are new but after a couple of washes they will soften up.

Bake-O-Glide is a great boon if you don't like washing up or cutting parchment to line cake tins. Bake-O-Glide is a reusable non-stick liner that simply needs a wash in hot soapy water after each use and will mean that tins only need a quick wash rather than a soak and scrub. This magic liner can be bought in a roll or, even easier, from the Aga shops you can get it as a set for all the Aga tins.

Apart from those essentials I have mentioned one or two other pieces of equipment throughout this book:

Baking tray. Several years ago Aga brought out a baking tray similar to the roasting tin. At first I couldn't see the reason to have a shallow tin when the roasting tin worked so well. Now I have to eat my words. I have the large and small size and use them practically every day. Because they are shallow roast vegetables, for example, cook faster and better than in the roasting tin. These tins of course fit on the oven runners. In some recipes in this book I have stated a shelf position. If you have the Aga tins use that runner or put the shelf on the runner suggested and your own tin on that.

The wok and the ridged pan. Aga now make a heavy wok with a flat base to make contact with the hotplate. To have a successful stir-fry it is essential that the wok is hot before you start cooking. Place the empty wok on the boiling plate for at least ten minutes, yes, ten minutes! During Aga demonstrations I know that the wok is getting hot because the audience shows signs of concern, expecting the whole thing to explode! When the wok is hot start cooking quickly as the oil will burn if you haven't got the ingredients ready to go in straight away. Similarly, the ridged pan. Choose one with deep ridges that can be heated well. Cast iron is the best, but heavy. There is never any need to put oil in these pans, anyway the oil would disappear into the base of the pan and be of no use. If you want to 'grill' vegetables, however, then brush them with oil before putting them in the pan. Again, you need to heat the pan for a minimum of ten minutes, and you can do this on the floor of the roasting oven if the pan handle is ovenproof.

A timer. This is essential as food cooking in the Aga will not be smelt, unless of course if you go in the garden! Try and obey the timer. I have two problems with timers. Firstly if I am busy when the timer rings I think I will check the ovens in a minute, and often don't! Secondly the timer rings and I can't think of anything in the oven so don't check! We have our fair share of charcoal dishes.

COOKING WITH THE AGA

You will have more success with your Aga if you understand the reasoning behind strange instructions like 'cooking potatoes in the oven'. The Aga uses stored heat. The ovens cook well when they are heated to their optimum temperature, your engineer will explain this, and will cook with a lovely even heat. As soon as the hotplate lids are lifted there is going to be some heat loss. Obviously this is not significant if just boiling a kettle or making toast, but cooking a pan of potatoes ready to mash will lower the oven temperature. So, always think, can this be done in the oven? The other advantage here is that you don't have pans boiling dry and steam and smells filling the kitchen.

To help keep the heat even in the Aga the lids on the hotplates are insulated and fairly heavy. Keep these lids down when not using the hotplates. The outer part of the lid is either chrome, stainless steel or cast iron. These will in time scratch so look after them. To non-Aga owners the boiling plate lid is the perfect place to put the kettle! Use a protective Chef's pad, folded tea towel or a trivet to protect the lids. I find that I don't use my hot plates very much. Boiling the kettle and making toast are the obvious examples. The boiling plate is also used to bring water to the boil, start vegetables or rice cooking, and of course wok cooking and making pancakes in a frying pan. The simmering plate is the place to make sauces, Welsh cakes and drop scones, toasted sandwiches and gravy.

Otherwise steaming, grilling and frying are usually done in the roasting oven. The ovens might look small from the outside but they are Tardis-like inside. The whole of the oven can be used as there is no single source of heat to spoil the food. It is not uncommon for the roasting oven to have an area where the food cooks marginally faster than the rest of the oven. All my gas Agas have been slightly hotter towards the back on the left-hand side of the roasting oven. This only causes a problem when doing large tray-bakes or trays of bread rolls, when turning the tray halfway through cooking usually solves that problem. All the ovens on an Aga, whether two or four are the same size. I once had a gentleman at a cookery demonstration who wished to see the room behind the Aga as he was convinced that I could not produce so much food from a two-oven Aga in the time. Needless to say he didn't manage to find the secret hatch to another cooker

COOKING TECHNIQUES

BOILED POTATOES AND ROOT VEGETABLES

Although explained in most recipes, this is a useful guideline. In fact, I can only give guidelines because cooking times vary according to the size and age of the vegetables and how well done you like them. If you cook them for more than 1½ hours I find they tend to taste dull. Use a pan that can be used in the simmering oven. Do not be tempted to put the vegetables in a serving dish after their initial boiling, the heat in the pan is needed to help cook the vegetables.

Pour 2.5 cm (1 inch) water into a saucepan and season with salt. Prepare the vegetables and put in the pan. Cover with a lid and bring them to the boil on the boiling plate. Boil for about 1 minute and then drain well. Return the vegetables to the pan, cover, and place in the simmering oven. Potatoes take about 40 minutes; carrots 15-20 minutes. Drain off any excess moisture and toss in butter.

One word of warning, the pan handles will be cold when you put them in the oven but very hot when you take them out, so remember to use gauntlets, and don't forget the lid handle will be hot as well!

RICE

I hear so many times that rice cooked in the Aga is the best ever. I think it is the easiest ever! For perfect results use a good quality rice – cheap varieties tend to become sticky.

Measure 1 cup of rice into a saucepan with a good pinch salt. Add 1½ cups of water. Cover and bring to the boil on the boiling plate. As soon as the water boils transfer the pan to the simmering oven. Cook for the following times, although they are a guideline:

Thai rice 8-10 minutes
Basmati rice 10 minutes
Long grain, white 12 minutes

Long grain, brown 25-30 minutes.

Stir the rice when cooked and drain off any excess moisture and then fluff it up with a fork. If the rice is ready and you are not, simply replace the lid, put the pan into the simmering oven and the rice will hold for an hour.

DRIED PEAS AND BEANS

The range of dried beans available in the shops gives a whole host of flavour, colour and texture to your cooking. Lentils of all variety do not need soaking, just washing, but all other pulses must be soaked for 8-12 hours and then rinsed with clean water.

After soaking and rinsing place the pulses in a pan that can be used in the simmering oven. Cover with cold water and bring to the boil. Boil rapidly for 10 minutes. Cover with a lid and transfer to the simmering oven until the pulses are cooked, which will vary between one and three hours.

COOKING PASTA

This can also be done in the oven, but I usually find that the cooking time is so short it isn't necessary to save heat. However, cooking in the oven prevents the pasta water boiling over and the kitchen filling with steam. Pasta doesn't really need a rolling boil to cook well and prevent sticking. (The reason for pasta sticking together is either due to over cooking or using cheap pasta.)

Bring a large pan of salted water to the boil on the boiling plate. Plunge in the pasta and bring to the boil. Move the pan to the floor of the roasting oven and cook for the time stated on the packet. Check a piece of pasta to see if it is al dente. Drain the pasta well and serve.

VEGETABLE STOCK

This is very easy to make in the Aga though we all resort to the instant variety some times. Home-made stock needs to be used within three days of being made or it can be frozen in useful quantities. Have a large saucepan and put into it a selection of vegetables, e.g. onions, carrots, leeks, celery. These need to be scrubbed clean or peeled and roughly chopped. Of course this is an excellent use for vegetable trimmings.

Cover the vegetables with water and add a bouquet garni and a few peppercorns. Season with salt. Cover with a lid and bring the contents to the boil on the boiling plate. Move to the simmering plate and bubble for about 10 minutes before transferring to the simmering oven for 2-3 hours. Strain the pan contents through a sieve, discarding the flavourless vegetables and herbs. Pack the stock into useful-sized containers and either chill or freeze it when cold. Use as a base for soups and sauces.

ROAST VEGETABLES

Either for traditional roast potatoes or as a fashionable way of cooking a variety of softer vegetables. Whichever, you will certainly appreciate their flavour. Aga roasting brings out the sweetness of these vegetables.

For main-crop potatoes peel and cut these to an even size. Place in a saucepan with about 2.5 cm (1 inch) of water in it and bring to the boil. Boil for 2-3 minutes and then drain well. Toss in vegetable oil, I find this easiest to do in the saucepan, and then tip the potatoes onto a shallow roasting tray or into a roasting tin. Hang the tin towards the top of the roasting oven and roast for about an hour, until the potatoes are crisp and golden brown. If the oven is very full the potatoes can be cooked on the floor of the oven, but they will need turning two or three times during cooking.

For new or salad potatoes I simply wash them well, cut to an even size and place on a baking tray. Drizzle over a little olive oil, toss well. Season with salt and add a sprig of rosemary. Place towards the top of the roasting oven and roast for about an hour. Remove the rosemary before serving.

For peppers, aubergines, etc., prepare as usual and cut into even-sized strips or chunks. Place on a roasting tray and drizzle over a little olive oil. Season with salt and roast towards the top of the roasting oven for about 40 minutes. The vegetables should be cooked with a slightly blackened tinge. Serve hot or cold.

USING YOUR AGA

All the following recipes give specific cooking instructions, so even if you are new to Aga ownership you should find getting to know your Aga fairly simple. But here are a few hints and tips to help you get the most from your Aga. I learn so much from meeting other Aga owners, those that come to spend the day with me doing a cookery course as well as all the customers I meet in Aga showrooms.

Whether or not your Aga is shiny new or a cherished older model a few basics will help you get the most from it. An Aga is really a storage heater that releases stored heat gently into the ovens. As soon as the lids are lifted then the stored heat will be used quickly, so the basic principle is to use the oven heat as much as possible. This is something that new owners find difficult at first. Try cooking rice or potatoes by the method described above and you will see that using the oven is simple and saves pans of water boiling over and steam filling the kitchen.

As there is no single source of heat in the oven, food can be placed against the sides and back of each oven. The floor of the roasting oven is useful to bake pastry cases on as well as pies, and you can put a frying pan on it for frying onions. As the ovens are fully vented there is no cross-flavouring of food being cooked together in the oven.

The two hotplates are also fairly versatile. The boiling plate is used to boil the kettle (pointing the spout towards the lid directs the steam onto the inside of the lid and helps to keep it clean) and pans of boiling water. Making toast, using the characteristic Aga toast bat, is also done on this plate. Pre-heating the bat before putting the bread in will help prevent the bread from sticking. The wok and ridged pan are heated and used on this plate also. The simmering plate is the place where sauces are made, toasted sandwiches are toasted, drop scones and naan breads are cooked. Do not be tempted to cook any food with a lot of fat in it directly on the metal plates, the fat will burn and any excess will run into the insulation.

Give these plates a regular brush with a wire brush to remove crumbs and boiled over food. These little bits can slow the cooking in a saucepan or the boiling of a kettle.

Wipe over the black enamel top after every use and it will remain in good condition. The occasional clean with a damp cloth and Astonish paste should keep the Aga looking clean. The shiny chrome or stainless steel lids can be cleaned with a stainless steel cleaner or Bar Keepers Friend.

More details on how to clean the Aga when it is off for servicing can be found in my *Traditional Aga Cookery Book*.

BREAKFASTS

CRUNCHY, NUTTY MUESLI

Muesli is a popular dish for breakfast, but a lot of the commercial varieties are too sweet. When you make your own, which takes very little time and effort, you can add your favourite ingredients. You may prefer standard rolled oats to the jumbo ones, for example. I like my muesli soaked with milk and left to chill overnight.

125ml/4fl oz maple syrup
1 tsp vanilla essence
500g/1lb 2oz jumbo oats
100g/3½oz wheatgerm or bran
100g/3½oz nuts, your choice
100g/3½oz sunflower seeds
100g/3½oz dried apricots
100g/3½oz dried apples or pears, chopped

Measure the maple syrup into a jug, add the vanilla essence and stand on the back of the Aga to allow the syrup to become runny and easier to mix in. In a large mixing bowl put the oats, wheatgerm, nuts and sunflower seeds. Next, add the dried fruits to the oat mixture. Stir well. Pour over the maple syrup and stir well.

Line two large baking trays with Bake-O-Glide and divide the mixture between them. For the two-oven Aga hang the tray on the bottom set of runners of the roasting oven and slide the cold shelf on the runner above. For the four-oven Aga hang the tray on the second set of runners from the bottom of the baking oven.

Bake for 10 minutes. Cool well before storing in a tin.

Spoon into bowls and serve with milk.

GRANOLA

This is a crunchy cereal, great with milk but also a good topping for fruit or yogurt.

150g/5½oz jumbo oats
100g/3½oz wheatgerm or bran
1 tbsp poppy seeds
25g/1oz pumpkin seeds
25g/1oz sunflower seeds
25g/1oz soft brown sugar
1 tsp ground cinnamon
100g/3½oz ready-to-eat dried fruit, e.g. cherries, cranberries

Mix together the oats, wheatgerm or bran, the poppy seeds, pumpkin seeds, sunflower seeds and the sugar in a mixing bowl. Tip the mixed dry ingredients onto a baking tray and spread out.

For a two-oven Aga hang the tray on the bottom set of runners of the roasting oven and slide in the cold shelf two runners above – for the four-oven Aga, hang the tray on the bottom set of runners of the baking oven.

Cook the granola for 10 minutes and then stir on the baking tray. Return to the oven for a further 10 minutes. Cool for a few minutes and add the cinnamon and fruit.

Allow to cool completely before storing in an airtight container.

To serve: spoon into a bowl and add milk.

TRADITIONAL OVERNIGHT PORRIDGE

This is a lovely traditional and nutritious dish that is easily made in the Aga. Over the last few years I have often been told that porridge made in the simmering oven is too thick and overcooked. I can only think that now porridge can be made in the microwave, the oats are more heavily rolled. So below is my solution – Aga overnight porridge!

1 mugful porridge oats
2 mugs milk or 1 mug milk and 1 mug water

To serve
Your choice of cream, milk, salt, soft brown sugar

Place the porridge oats and the milk, or milk and water, together in a saucepan and cover with a lid. Stand on the back of the Aga overnight.

In the morning stand the pan on the simmering plate and stir for one to two minutes until piping hot. Serve with one of the toppings.

Serves 2

APPLE PORRIDGE

This is a variation on standard porridge, using apple juice instead of milk and fruit instead of sugar.

1 mugful porridge oats
2 mugs apple juice
1 eating apple, grated
2 tbsp sultanas

Measure the porridge oats into a saucepan and add the apple juice. Cover with a lid and stand at the back of the Aga overnight.

In the morning move the pan to the simmering plate and stir the porridge for a minute or two until the porridge is piping hot. Stir in the sultanas and serve with the grated apple on top.

Serves 2

LANCASHIRE EGGS

A variation on the theme of scrambled egg. Lancashire cheese is easy to use because it crumbles and doesn't need a grater. Alternatively Caerphilly, Cheshire and Wensleydale can be used. These cheeses also have fairly mild flavours that work well with the eggs.

2 eggs, beaten
2 tbsp milk
salt and pepper
25g/1oz Lancashire cheese, crumbled
15g/1/2oz butter

In a basin mix together the eggs, milk, salt and pepper and the Lancashire cheese. Melt the butter in a small saucepan on the simmering plate and add the egg mixture. Stir gently until scrambled.

Serve immediately on toast.

Serves 2

GLAMORGAN SAUSAGES

These are just cheese sausages, not like the 'vegetarian' sausages sold in the supermarkets. These hold together much better when cooking if they have had plenty of time to chill. I usually make them the day before I need them. It also allows the flavours to develop.

175g/6oz fresh white breadcrumbs
100g/3½oz Caerphilly cheese, grated
3 spring onions, finely chopped
1 tbsp finely chopped parsley
pinch mustard powder or ½ tsp mustard
salt and pepper
2 eggs, 1 whole and 1 separated
about 60ml/4 tbsp milk
plain flour for coating
1 tbsp vegetable oil
25g/1oz butter

In a large mixing bowl put the breadcrumbs, cheese, onion, parsley, mustard and a seasoning of salt and pepper. Mix very well and then add 1 egg, beaten and 1 egg yolk. Continue to mix and add enough milk to bind the mixture together.

Divide the mixture into 8 portions and roll each portion into a sausage shape.

Put the remaining egg white in a bowl and beat until frothy. Pour the beaten egg white onto a plate. Place some flour onto another plate. Coat the sausages with egg white and then roll in the flour. Brush off any excess flour.

Heat the oil and butter in a frying pan and fry the sausages for 8-10 minutes, until hot through and golden brown.

Makes 8 sausages

POTATO SCONES

These potato scones make a good breakfast dish and can be made in advance, though they may loose a fraction of their lightness in doing so. Freshly cooked potatoes work best, but there is no reason why you can't use left-over potato. Choose Pentland Squire or Maris Piper potatoes for the best mash.

450g/1lb potatoes, peeled
1 teaspoon salt
25g/1oz butter
110g/4oz plain flour, approximately

Cut the potatoes into large dice and place in a saucepan with 2.5cm/ 1 inch of water in the bottom. Cover the pan and bring to the boil. Boil the potatoes for 1-2 minutes and then drain off all the water. Place the covered pan in the simmering oven for 30-40 minutes, or until the potatoes are cooked enough to mash. Drain off any remaining water.

Mash the potatoes with the salt and butter and then work in enough flour to make a stiff dough. Turn onto a floured worksurface and knead the dough until smooth. Roll or pat out to a circle 0.5cm/¼- inch thick. Cut into 8 triangles.

Brush the simmering plate to remove any carbon and then oil lightly. Place the potato scones on the plate and cook until golden brown and then turn over and brown the other side, about 4-5 minutes each side.

Serve hot with butter.

Makes 8

DATE MUFFINS

These muffins are of the American variety. They are at their best when still warm from the oven and make a useful addition to breakfasts. The ingredients can be measured the night before and the liquid added when you are ready to bake them.

225g/8oz wholemeal flour
pinch of salt
1 tsp baking powder
75g/2³/₄oz chopped dates
2 eggs
100g/3¹/₂oz plain yogurt
200ml/7fl oz milk
100g/3¹/₂oz runny honey
100ml/3¹/₂fl oz light vegetable oil

Line with paper muffin cases or butter 12 deep muffin tins.

Place the flour, salt and baking powder in a mixing bowl and stir. Then add the chopped dates and stir again.

Place the eggs in a basin and beat with a fork and then add the yogurt, milk, honey and vegetable oil. Pour into the dry ingredients and stir well to incorporate all the flour. The mixture will be quite soft.

Spoon the mixture into the muffin tins.

Hang the oven shelf on the third set of runners from the top of the roasting oven and bake for 12-15 minutes, until risen and firm to the touch.

Makes 12

SODA BREAD

Another recipe that can be made quickly for breakfast, or indeed as an accompaniment for all sorts of dishes.

350g/12oz wholemeal flour
100g/3¹/₂ oz plain white flour
1 tsp salt
1 tsp bicarbonate soda
50g/1³/₄ oz butter
225ml/8 fl oz milk
150g/5¹/₂ oz plain yogurt
flour to dust

Mix the flours, salt and bicarbonate of soda together in a mixing bowl. Rub in the butter until the mixture resembles breadcrumbs. Add the milk and yogurt to make a firm dough

Place the dough on a lightly floured worktop and knead the dough until smooth. Shape the dough into a flat circular shape. Place on a floured baking tray and cut a cross right across the dough. Dust with flour.

Hang the tray on the third set of runners from the top of the roasting oven for 30-35 minutes, until the bread is crusty and golden brown and sounds hollow when tapped underneath. Cool on a wire rack.

SOUPS

ASPARAGUS SOUP

A good way of using the left over trimmings from the *Cheese and Asparagus Tart* recipe on page 86. Use a few asparagus tips for garnish.

225g/8oz asparagus
25g/1oz butter
1 onion, finely chopped
450ml/³⁄₄ pint vegetable stock
150ml/¹⁄₄ pint single cream
salt and pepper

Trim and steam the asparagus until cooked through. Melt the butter in a saucepan and sauté the onion until soft but not browning. Chop the asparagus stalks and add to the onion, reserving the tips for garnishing. Add the stock and bring to the boil. Place the pan in the simmering oven and cook for 25-30 minutes.

Liquidise the contents of the pan. Rinse the pan and return the soup to it. Heat through and adjust the seasoning. Stir in the asparagus tips and serve garnished with the cream.

Serves 4

CURRIED SWEET POTATO SOUP

Sweet potatoes can be expensive to buy but worth it because they taste so good and have a wonderful colour. The combination of the potatoes, banana and spices gives this a Caribbean flavour.

1 tbsp vegetable oil
1 onion, peeled and chopped
2 cloves garlic, peeled and crushed
2 tbsp curry paste
2 large sweet potatoes, peeled and chopped
1 large courgette, chopped
4 tomatoes, chopped
1l/1³/₄ pints vegetable stock
1 banana, peeled and chopped
2 large naan breads (see page 106)

You will need a large saucepan to make this soup.

Heat the oil in the saucepan and add the onion. Cook gently until the onion is soft but not coloured. Add the garlic and cook for 1-2 minutes and then stir in the curry paste. Keep stirring and cook for another 1-2 minutes. Add the sweet potatoes, courgettes and tomatoes to the paste mixture and turn until well coated.

Pour over the stock, stir well and bring to the boil. Cover with a lid and transfer to the simmering oven for 30-40 minutes, until the sweet potatoes are soft. Add the chopped bananas and cook for a further 5-10 minutes.

Blend the soup and adjust the seasoning.

Toast the naan breads on the simmering plate for 1-2 minutes on each side and then cut into slices to serve with the soup.

Serves 4-6

CELERIAC AND STILTON SOUP

Many people tell me they don't know what to do with this knobbly looking vegetable. It can be sliced into sticks and eaten raw and it imparts a lovely celery flavour but without that slightly stringy texture.

1.5kg/3lb 5oz celeriac
1 tbsp lemon juice
50g/2oz butter
2 onions, peeled and chopped
1 clove garlic, peeled and crushed
2l/3½ pints vegetable stock
2 tbsp light vegetable oil
350g/12oz blue Stilton
150ml/¼ pint double cream
salt and pepper

Peel the celeriac and cut off one slice. Cut this piece into fine chips and toss in the lemon juice. Set aside.

Roughly chop the remaining celeriac. Melt the butter in a large saucepan and add the onions. Cook gently until softening but not browning. Add the celeriac and cook gently for a further 5 minutes and then stir in the garlic. Add the stock and cover with a lid. Bring to the boil and then transfer to the simmering oven for 40-50 minutes, until the vegetables are soft enough to blend.

While the soup is cooking dry the celeriac chips and fry in the oil until crisp. Drain on kitchen paper.

Blend the soup and return to the pan and heat through. Crumble the Stilton in and stir until melting and then add the cream. When the Stilton is fully melted, check the seasoning. Serve in warmed bowls garnished with the celeriac chips.

Makes 8

PARSNIP AND APPLE SOUP

This creamy soup is perfect for a cold winter's day when parsnips are at their best.

700g/1½lb parsnips, peeled and chopped
25g/1oz butter
1 large cooking apple, e.g. Bramley, peeled, cored and
roughly chopped
1.2l/2 pints vegetable stock
4 fresh sage leaves
2 cloves
salt and pepper
150ml/¼ pint single cream
a few fresh sage leaves to garnish

Melt the butter in a large saucepan. Add the parsnips and toss in the butter. Cook for 5 minutes and then add the apples. Cook for a further 5 minutes and then add the stock, sage leaves and cloves. Stir well, cover and bring to the boil.

When boiling move the pan to the simmering oven and allow to cook for 40-50 minutes, until the parsnips are tender.

Remove the sage leaves and the cloves and blend the soup until smooth. Stir in the cream and adjust the seasoning.

Serve in warm bowls garnished with sage leaves.

Serves 6

BROAD BEAN SOUP

As a child we seemed to have a lot of broad beans from the garden and I hated them. Now I love them! This soup can be made with frozen beans and peas, which will need less cooking.

225g/8oz shelled broad beans
225g/8oz podded peas
1 large onion, peeled and finely chopped
425ml/³/₄ pint milk
300ml/¹/₂ pint vegetable stock
salt and pepper

Place the broad beans, peas, onion, milk and vegetable stock in a large saucepan. Bring to the boil, cover and then place in the simmering oven for 25-30 minutes, until the beans are tender.

For a chunky soup, just purée half the soup in a blender, for a smoother soup purée all the soup. Return the soup to the pan and season to taste.

Heat through and serve with crispy croûtons.

Serves 4

Pea and Spinach Soup

This is a quick and easy soup to make with a wonderful fresh flavour. If you like really smooth soups you can pass the soup through a sieve after it has been blended.

50g/2oz butter
1 large potato, peeled and diced
2 sticks celery, scrubbed and chopped
125ml/¼ pint white wine
1l/1¾ pint vegetable stock
500g/1lb 2oz frozen peas
100g/4oz spinach, well washed, stalks removed
pinch of sugar
1 tbsp chopped parsley of mint
salt and pepper

Heat the butter in a large saucepan, add the diced potato and celery and toss them in the butter. Cover with a lid and cook for 4-5 minutes until the vegetables are softening but not browning.

Pour the wine into the saucepan and bubble the mixture until the wine has reduced by half. Pour in the vegetable stock and then add the peas and the spinach leaves. Bring to the boil, replace the cover and put into the simmering oven for 30 minutes. Remove the pan from the oven and stir in the sugar and chopped herbs.

Pour the soup into a blender, rinse the pan out and pour the puréed soup back into the pan. Adjust the seasoning, heat through and serve either with a little cream or crunchy croûtons.

Serves 6

LETTUCE AND WATERCRESS SOUP

A great way to use those surplus lettuces from the garden. Although this is primarily a soup to serve chilled, I have served it hot when the weather has been on the chilly side.

25g/1oz butter
1 onion, peeled and finely chopped
1 medium potato, peeled and finely chopped
1l/1³/₄ pints vegetable stock
1 round lettuce, washed
1 bunch watercress, washed, remove stalks
salt and pepper
150ml/¹/₄ pint single cream
chives, chopped to garnish

Melt the butter in a roomy saucepan and sauté the onion until soft but not coloured. Add the potatoes and toss them in the butter and then pour in the stock. Bring to the boil and cover with a lid.

Move to the simmering oven and cook for 15-20 minutes. When the potato is cooked move the pan to the simmering plate and add the lettuce, torn into pieces and the watercress. Bring to the boil and remove from the heat.

Blend the soup and pour into a bowl to chill. Adjust seasoning. Just before serving, stir in the cream and garnish with chopped chives.

Serves 6

CHESTNUT SOUP

This is a good way to use those cans of chestnut purée that seem to gather over time in the cupboard! Chestnut soup is of course a good Christmas dish.

1 tbsp vegetable oil
1 onion, peeled and chopped
2 sticks celery, chopped
600ml/1 pint water
1 bouquet garni
salt and pepper
1 can (439g)/16 oz unsweetened chestnut purée
300ml/1/2 pint milk
1-2 tsp lemon juice

Heat the oil in a saucepan and sauté the onion and celery until soft but not browned. Add the water, bouquet garni and salt and pepper. Bring to the boil and place in the simmering oven for 10 minutes, to allow the flavours to infuse.

Return to the simmering plate and add the chestnut purée and the milk. Whilst heating through stir well to allow the chestnut purée to blend in. Bubble for 1-2 minutes and then remove the bouquet garni.

Blend the soup and add enough lemon juice to take off the very rich edge.

Heat through and serve with fresh crusty bread.

Serves 6

ROAST TOMATO SOUP WITH CROÛTONS AND BASIL PURÉE

This soup is good to make if tomatoes are cheap at the greengrocer or market. It would be a waste to use tasty tomatoes that you have grown or paid a premium price for. The roasting will help the flavour along.

2kg/4½ lb tomatoes
4 sticks celery, sliced
6-8 cloves garlic, peeled
1 small bulb fennel, sliced
thyme, sprig
rosemary, large stalk
4 bay leaves
6 tbsp olive oil
salt and pepper
1 tbsp tomato purée
juice of 1 lemon
½ tsp sugar

Cut the tomatoes in half and place on a baking tray with the celery, garlic and fennel. Lay the herbs on top of the vegetables and drizzle over the olive oil. Season with salt. Hang the tray on the top set of runners of the roasting oven and roast for 20 minutes. Remove from the oven and stir the vegetables around. Return to the oven for a further 10-15 minutes, until the vegetables are cooked.

Tip the vegetables into a blender or processor along with the tomato purée, lemon juice, a seasoning of salt and pepper and the sugar. Blend the vegetables together, adding water to help the mixture along. Pass through a sieve into a saucepan and adjust the seasoning, adding more water if necessary. Heat through and serve with the croûtons and basil purée.

For the Croûtons

These can be made from any sort of bread such as a white loaf, ciabatta or baguette. Firstly, cut the bread into cubes and then pop them into a plastic bag and pour on some olive oil, a little at a time. Shake the bag between each addition of oil. I add enough oil to make the bread just moist. Then tip the bread onto a shallow baking tray and 'toast' at the top of the roasting oven for 10 minutes, remove the tray and stir the croûtons. Return to the oven for a further 5 minutes until toasted evenly.

Use immediately or when cold, store in an airtight container.

For the Basil Purée

50g/2oz basil leaves
¹/₂ tsp coarse salt
4 tbsp good olive oil
2 tsp balsamic vinegar

You can use a pestle and mortar or blender to make this.

In a pestle and mortar, pound the leaves and the salt together until smooth. Mix in the oil and balsamic vinegar. Stir well.

If using a blender put all the ingredients together and whizz until the leaves are well chopped.

To serve, spoon a little purée onto the top of the soup before serving.

Serves 4

STARTERS, SNACKS AND LIGHT LUNCHES

PANCAKES

Pancakes are so often only made on Shrove Tuesday. This is a shame as they are so good for wrapping round tasty savoury fillings. You can easily ring the changes by adding different herbs or flours to the batter. Once you get the hang of these, experiment with any fillings you like.

Making pancakes – a few tips

Try to use a heavy-based pan for pancakes. I have tried frying pans of all different types, and the most reliable has been my Berndes cast aluminum pan with a non-stick lining. An added bonus with this pan is that the handle can be detached for use in the oven.

....

This recipe for pancakes uses white plain flour, you can use wholemeal or buckwheat, but you will probably need to add a little more liquid. If the batter is allowed to stand for some time the batter will thicken and you may need to add a little more liquid.

Basic Batter

110g/4oz plain flour
pinch salt
1 egg, beaten
300ml/¹/₂ pint milk
oil for frying

Either place the flour, salt, egg and milk in a food processor and whizz to a batter or place the flour and salt in a mixing bowl and gradually beat in the egg and the milk slowly to make a smooth batter. The batter should be the consistency of thick cream.

This mixture will make about 12 pancakes, depending upon the size of your pan.

Cooking Pancakes

Heat a large solid-based pan on the boiling plate. Pour in a little oil and wipe it round with a wad of kitchen paper. Spoon in 2-3 tablespoons of batter and swirl around the pan. Cook for about a minute; lift the edge with a palette knife, and once it starts to brown underneath toss the pancake over and cook the second side for about 1 minute. Serve on a warm plate or keep hot in the simmering oven. Re-grease the pan after 2-3 pancakes.

The plain pancakes can be frozen, interleave each one with a sheet of greaseproof paper or cling film and wrap in a bag. Thaw as needed.

Fill with one of the following suggested fillings.

NORMANDY PANCAKES

1 quantity pancake batter mix
350g/12oz spinach, leaves only
2 tomatoes, skinned and chopped
150ml/¼ pint crème fraîche
pinch grated nutmeg
salt and pepper
25g/1oz butter, melted

Make the pancakes as per the recipe on page 44. Keep warm on a plate.

Wash the spinach and place in a saucepan. Cover with a lid and cook on the simmering plate until the spinach has wilted. Drain well, return to the pan and chop roughly.

Lay the pancakes on a work surface and spread each one with the crème fraîche followed by a layer of spinach. Grate over a little nutmeg and top with the tomatoes. Season with salt and pepper.

Roll up the pancakes and lay in a buttered shallow ovenproof dish. Brush the top with melted butter.

Put the shelf on the bottom set of runners of the roasting oven, slide in the pancakes and cook to heat through, about 15 minutes.

Serve with salsa or salad.

Serves 4

CHIVE PANCAKES WITH VEGETABLES AND CASHEWS

1 quantity pancake batter mix (see page 44)
2 tbsp chopped chives
1 tbsp sesame seed oil
1 tbsp light sunflower oil
2 tbsp light soy sauce
1 tbsp rice wine
1 tbsp tomato ketchup
half a cauliflower, broken into small florets
1 small head broccoli, broken into small florets,
stalk finely chopped
2 spring onions, finely chopped
2 carrots, peeled and cut into thin strips
110g/4oz mange tout, trimmed and cut into strips
110g/4oz cashew nuts
25g/1oz butter, melted

Stir the chopped chives into the pancake batter and make the pancakes as above. Keep warm. Heat the wok on the boiling plate for approximately 8-10 minutes. Meanwhile mix together the sesame oil and the sunflower oil, set aside and then mix together the rice wine, the soy sauce and the tomato ketchup.

Pour the oils into the wok and immediately add the cauliflower, broccoli, onions and carrots. Stir-fry for 2-3 minutes and then add the mange tout. Continue to cook for 3 or 4 minutes more and then add the soy sauce mixture and the cashew nuts. Heat through and set aside.

Place a spoonful of vegetable mixture on each pancake and roll up. Put the pancakes in a buttered shallow ovenproof dish. Pour over the melted butter. Put the oven shelf on the third set of runners from the top of the roasting oven and bake for 10-15 minutes, just enough to heat through.

Serves 4

ASPARAGUS FILLING

A perfect early summer dish, light enough for a starter or lunch dish. Any asparagus stalks not used in the pancake can be used for soup (see my recipe on page 32).

1 quantity pancake mix (see page 44)
2 tbsp parsley, chopped
24 asparagus spears
50g/2oz butter
50g/2oz Parmesan cheese, grated
50g/2oz Gruyère cheese, grated
salt and pepper

Make the pancake batter and stir in the chopped parsley. Set aside. Bring a pan of water to the boil, add a pinch of salt and plunge in the asparagus for 1-2 minutes, until just cooked and still bright green. Drain well.

Make eight pancakes, setting each one aside to keep warm as you make them.

Onto each pancake lay three asparagus spears, dot with butter and roll up. Place in a shallow buttered ovenproof dish. Scatter the grated cheeses over the pancakes.

Place the shelf on the second set of runners from the top of the roasting oven, place the pancake dish in the oven until the pancakes have heated through and the cheese has just begun to melt, no longer as the pancakes will dry out.

Serves 4

BLUE CHEESE PANCAKES

These pancakes have a very rich filling, so they are best served with plain vegetables or a salad. They really lend themselves to advance preparation, so are excellent for entertaining. Any blue cheese works well, but if blue's not to your liking you can use Wensleydale, which I particularly like.

250g/8oz blue cheese
75g/3oz butter, softened
50g/2oz plain flour
1 quantity of basic pancake batter (see page 44)
1 tbsp parsley chopped
200ml/7fl oz crème fraîche

Crumble the cheese into a mixing bowl and add the butter. Mix together well with a fork and then add the flour. Mix well. Place the cheese mixture onto a sheet of cling film and roll to a sausage. Chill well.

Divide the cheese sausage into 16 portions. Lay two pieces onto each pancake and then roll up the pancakes. Lay in a shallow, buttered ovenproof dish. Pour over the crème fraîche.

Bake for 15-20 minutes with the shelf on the second set of runners from the bottom of the roasting oven, until piping hot.

Serves 4

CRÊPE PURSES

These vegetable pancakes make an attractive dinner party starter. Reasonably sized pancakes are easier to shape although you may need an extra pair of hands when tying them up! These can be made a few hours in advance and chilled, before the final heating through.

1 quantity basic pancake batter (see page 44)
3 medium carrots, peeled and finely diced
1 small head of broccoli, broken into small florets
6 x 20-cm/8-inch strips of either leek or spring onion green
for tying
2 tbsp butter
1 small onion, peeled and finely chopped
2 stalks celery, finely diced
50g/2oz butter
1 tsp curry paste
3 tbsp plain flour
225ml/8 fl oz vegetable stock
150g/5oz thawed frozen peas
150g/5oz thawed corn kernels
salt and pepper
50g/2oz butter, melted

Make up a batch of pancakes, cover and set aside.

Bring a pan of lightly salted water to the boil. Plunge in the carrots and boil for 2 minutes. Remove with a slotted spoon and drain well. Next plunge in the broccoli florets and boil for 3 minutes, remove with a slotted spoon and drain. Then add the green strips to the boiling water and blanch for one minute. Drain well.

In a small saucepan melt the butter and sauté the onion until soft but not browning. Add the curry paste, keep stirring and cook for another 2 minutes. Stir in the flour, mix well and cook for a further minute. Gradually work in the stock and bubble well to make a thick sauce. Adjust the seasoning.

In a bowl put the carrots, broccoli, peas and corn and pour over the sauce. Stir gently to mix.

Lay out the pancakes and divide the vegetable filling between them, heaping it into the middle. Draw the edges of the pancake up around the filling and tie with the strips of spring onion or leek.

Brush the purses with the melted butter and place on a lightly buttered baking tray. Put the shelf on the bottom set of runners of the roasting oven and slide in the tray. Cook for 15-20 minutes, until the edges are crisp and golden and the purses are piping hot.

Serve hot.

Serves 6

AUBERGINE PANCAKES WITH FRESH TOMATO SAUCE

These little pancakes can be cooked directly on the simmering plate. The addition of pine nuts adds flavour and texture. Serve with a fresh tomato sauce and green salad for a light and easy lunch.

1 medium aubergine
50g/2oz plain flour
2 eggs
1 tbsp vegetable oil
1 tbsp lemon juice
1 clove garlic, peeled and crushed
50g/2oz pine nuts
1 small onion, peeled and finely chopped
good pinch of salt
pepper

Cut the aubergine in half lengthways and place on a baking tray, cut side uppermost. Put the shelf on the second set of runners from the top of the roasting oven and slide in the aubergine tray. Bake for 15-20 minutes, until the flesh aubergine is soft when pierced with a knife. Leave until cool enough to handle and then scoop out all the flesh into a processor or blender. Add the flour to the aubergine and purée.

Then add the eggs, oil and lemon juice. Whizz to make a smooth batter. Add the garlic and onion and give one short burst on the processor. Stir in the pine nuts and a seasoning of salt and pepper.

Brush the simmering plate to remove any carbonised debris and then rub with a little vegetable oil on a wad of kitchen paper. Spoon a tablespoon of batter on to the simmering plate and level off. You will probably get four pancakes on the plate at a time. Cook until the underside is golden brown and then turn over to cook the second side, about 2 minutes. Re-grease and continue to cook the remaining batter. Keep the cooked pancakes warm in the simmering oven on a tray in a single layer while cooking all the remaining batter.

Makes between 12 and 15 pancakes

Fresh Tomato Sauce

1kg/2¼ lb fresh tomatoes, as ripe as possible
1 onion, peeled and chopped finely
3 cloves garlic, peeled and crushed
2 tbsp olive oil
good sprig of thyme
basil leaves, handful
salt and pepper

Place the tomatoes in a large bowl and pour over boiling water. Peel the skins off and cut the tomatoes in half. Remove the core and the seeds and cut the flesh into small dice. Place in a saucepan along with the remaining ingredients. Bring to a gentle bubble on the simmering plate and move to the simmering oven for 30 minutes. Do not cover with a lid. This will allow the sauce to thicken. Stir well and serve with the pancakes.

CHEESE, BASIL AND PINENUT TRIANGLES

Serve these as part of a selection of nibbles instead of a formal starter.

110g/4oz butter
110g/4oz feta cheese
110g/4oz ricotta cheese
2 tbsp freshly chopped basil leaves
3 tbsp pinenuts, toasted
1 egg, beaten
salt and pepper
14 sheets filo pastry(the quantity will vary according to the type you buy, they all come in varying sizes!)

Place the butter in a basin and stand at the back of the Aga to melt or place in a small saucepan and melt over a low heat on the hob.

Mix together the cheeses, basil, pinenuts and the egg, season to taste.

Lay a sheet of filo pastry on the worktop and brush with melted butter. Lay a second sheet of filo pastry on top and cut the pastry into four long strips. Each strip will make one triangle.

Place two teaspoons of the cheese mixture at the base of one strip and fold the pastry over diagonally to form a triangle. Then repeat with two more sheets of pastry until all of the filling has been used. Continue to fold up the length of the pastry enclosing the filling. Place on a buttered baking tray and continue until all the filling and the pastry have been used.

Brush the triangles with melted butter and bake on the third set of runners from the top of the roasting oven for 15 minutes, until crisp and golden brown. Serve hot.

Variation on the filling

Sauté a small, finely chopped onion with a crushed clove garlic in 1 tbsp olive oil until soft. Add two finely chopped red chillies. Cook for 1 minute. Drain a 400g/14oz-can of kidney beans and mash them. Add the onion mixture and 1 tablespoon of ready-made tomato salsa (see page 69). Use this mixture to fill the filo pastry and continue as above.

Makes about 28

ROAST PEPPER TARTLETS

The peppers and tomatoes give these tartlets a lovely mediterranean flavour.

2 red peppers, cored and seeded
2 green peppers, cored and seeded
salt and pepper
3 tbsp olive oil
375g-pack ready-rolled puff pastry
2 tbsp grainy mustard
2 tbsp tomato purée
8 cherry tomatoes

Cut the peppers into strips and place on a shallow baking tray. Drizzle over the olive oil and season with salt and pepper. Hang the tin on the second set of runners from the top of the roasting oven and roast the peppers for 25-30 minutes, until softened.

Unroll the pastry onto a large baking tray and cut into eight rectangles.

Mix together the mustard and the tomato purée. Spread this mixture over the middle of each rectangle, leaving a border.

Quarter the cherry tomatoes and divide these between the pastry rectangles along with the roast peppers.

Hang the tray on the second set of runners from the top of the roasting oven for 10-15 minutes, until the pastry has risen and become golden brown. Move the tray to the floor of the roasting oven for 5 minutes to crisp the base of the pastry.

Serve hot.

Makes 8

Couscous, Tomato and Haloumi Salad

This is a warm salad. The couscous can be prepared in advance and the cheese cooked at the last minute. Choose a pan that can be used on the floor of the roasting oven and you won't have any mess on the top of the Aga or in the kitchen.

225g/8oz couscous
3 tbsp olive oil
salt and pepper
600ml/1 pint boiling water
1 red onion, peeled and thinly sliced
250g/9oz haloumi
12 baby plum tomatoes, halved
2 cloves garlic, peeled and sliced
75g/3oz olives, a mixture of green and black
1 tbsp parsley, chopped
parsley, sprigs to garnish
lemon wedges

Place the couscous and 1 tablespoon of olive oil in a bowl, season with salt and pepper. Pour over the boiling water. Stand at the back of the Aga until the water has been absorbed then fluff up with a fork.

Heat another tablespoon of the oil in a frying pan and fry the onion until softening. Remove to a plate and keep warm. Pour the remaining tablespoon of olive oil in the pan and fry the slices of haloumi for 2 to 3 minutes on each side. Add the tomato halves and garlic slices and toss in the pan juices for 1-2 minutes, just to coat but not to cook the tomatoes as they need to keep their shape. Add the olives and the reserved onions and season with salt and pepper.

Stir chopped parsley into the couscous and divide out onto plates. Top with haloumi slices and the pan contents. Serve with lemon wedges.

Serves 4

FELAFEL WITH TOMATO SALSA

These popular chickpea balls can be eaten hot or cold. It is essential to chill them well before frying to help form a good shape, and so be sure to allow plenty of time for the preparation. I like to use my wok for the deep-frying.

400g/14oz chickpeas, soaked for 4 hours or overnight.
1 small onion, peeled and finely chopped
2 cloves garlic, peeled and crushed
2 tbsp parsley, chopped
1 tbsp coriander, chopped
2 tsp ground cumin
1 tbsp water
1/2 tsp baking powder
vegetable oil for frying

Drain the soaked chickpeas and place in a food processor. Blend until the chickpeas are finely ground. Add the onion, garlic, parsley, coriander, cumin, water and baking powder. Whizz to make a rough paste. Turn into a bowl and cover. Leave to stand for 30 minutes.

Take tablespoons of the mixture and squeeze out any excess water. Roll into balls. Chill.

Heat enough oil in a pan to be half the depth of each felafel ball. To test if the oil is the right temperature, drop a cube of bread into the oil and if it floats quickly to the top and turns golden brown then it is hot enough to fry the felafel.

Fry the felafel balls, turning in the oil, until brown all round. Remove with a slotted spoon and drain on kitchen paper.

Serve hot or cold with tomato salsa.

Serves 4

MIXED BEAN SALAD

This is a quick bean salad using those faithful cans of beans lurking, forgotten, in the dark recesses of your store cupboard.

400g/14oz-can red kidney beans
400g/14oz-can flageolet beans
200g/7oz-can sweetcorn
1 spring onion, trimmed and finely chopped
4 button mushrooms, finely sliced
1 tbsp olive oil
1 tbsp balsamic vinegar
2 tbsp extra virgin olive oil
fresh parsley, a few sprigs, chopped

Drain the cans of beans and sweetcorn and rinse in cold water. Drain well. Tip into a serving bowl.

Heat the olive oil in a small saucepan and fry the mushrooms briefly, then add the onions and cook for 1 minute. Add this mixture to the beans.

Whisk together the balsamic vinegar and olive oil and pour over the bean mixture. Mix well. Scatter over the parsley.

Serves 6-8

CAULIFLOWER SOUFFLÉ

Cauliflower is so often a good buy at the greengrocer and I find it a very versatile vegetable. I love it raw in salads or just for nibbles but this recipe is also delicious and isn't any more difficult than the perennial favourite, cauliflower cheese. Take care not to overcook the cauliflower.

225g/8oz cauliflower florets
salt and pepper
50g/2oz butter
3 tbsp flour
200ml/7fl oz milk
1 tbsp wholegrain mustard
100g/4oz mature Cheddar cheese, grated
4 eggs, separated

Butter well eight ramekin dishes. You may prefer to make one large soufflé, in which case butter a 1.5l/1/3 pint soufflé dish. Bring a pan of salted water to the boil and plunge in the cauliflower. Cook until tender and drain well.

Put the butter, flour and milk in a saucepan. Stand on the simmering plate and whisk well until a smooth sauce has formed. Add the mustard and a seasoning of salt and pepper. Pour the sauce into a blender or processor and add the cauliflower. Whizz until smooth. Pour into a bowl and stir in the grated cheese and egg yolks. Whisk the egg whites in a separate bowl until stiff and gently stir one tablespoon of the egg white into the sauce. Carefully fold in the remaining egg whites.

Divide the mixture between the prepared ramekins and stand on a baking tray. Bake on the third set of runners from the top of the roasting oven until risen and golden brown – 20-25 minutes for individual ones or 35-40 minutes for a large soufflé. Serve immediately.

Serves 8 as a starter or 4 as a main course

CHEESY POTATO SOUFFLÉ

This is a just a smart name for a smart cheese and potato pie. Cheese and potato pie was popular when I started teaching what was then known as Domestic Science, however I always thought it looked too dull a dish for the children to proudly take home with them after class. But cooked in this way using a mature, unpasteurised Cheddar gives flavour whilst using a cheese such as Red Leicester or Cotswold with its chives and onions will give not only flavour but also colour.

1kg/2lb 4oz potatoes
50g/2oz butter
125ml/¼ pint milk
2 eggs, separated
1 tsp mustard
175g/6oz firm cheese, such as mature Cheddar, grated
salt and pepper

Peel the potatoes and cut them all to an even size. Put them in a large saucepan filled with 2.5cm/1 inch of water. Season with salt. Cover with a lid and stand on the boiling plate and bring the pan to a rapid boil. Boil well for 1 minute and then drain off all the water.

Replace the lid and put the pan of potatoes in the simmering oven for 50-60 minutes. Because no water is needed in the pan they won't become waterlogged and collapse. Prod the potatoes to see if they are soft enough to mash. Drain any moisture from the pan.

Add the butter to the potatoes and start mashing them, gradually adding the milk as the potatoes break down. When the potatoes are mashed stir in the mustard, egg yolks and grated cheese. Season to taste.

Whisk the egg whites to a medium white-peak stage. Add one tablespoon of the egg white to the potatoes and beat in. Fold in the remaining egg white.

Butter a 1.5-l/2¾-pint soufflé dish. Spoon in the potato mixture. Place the oven shelf on the bottom set of runners of the roasting oven. Slide in the soufflé dish and bake the potato soufflé for 20-25 minutes, until risen and golden brown.

Serves 4-6

SAGE DERBY SOUFFLÉS

These individual soufflés are so simple to make but you do need everyone sitting at the table ready to eat them straight from the oven. If you can't find Sage Derby cheese then a good farmhouse Cheddar with some finely chopped sage leaves will do.

300ml/1/2 pint milk
50g/2oz flour
50g/2oz butter
salt and pepper
3 eggs, separated
75g/3oz Sage Derby cheese, grated

Butter well 6 individual ramekin dishes. Stand on a baking tray.

In a saucepan place the milk, flour, butter and a seasoning of salt and pepper. Stand the saucepan on the simmering plate and whisk the mixture to make a smooth, glossy thick sauce. Remove from the heat and stir in the cheese. When the cheese has melted beat in the egg yolks.

In a clean bowl whisk the egg whites until white and fluffy. Place 1 tablespoonful in the pan with the sauce and beat in. Pour the sauce into the egg whites and gently fold to combine the mixture. Spoon this soufflé mixture into the buttered ramekins. Wipe around the edge of each ramekin to ensure the soufflé will rise evenly.

For a two-oven Aga put the shelf on the floor of the roasting oven and slide in the tray of soufflés. Put the cold shelf on the second set of runners from the top. For a four-oven Aga put the shelf on the bottom set of runners in the baking oven and slide in the tray of soufflés.

Bake for 25-30 minutes until the soufflés are risen and golden brown. (If you need to open the oven door during the cooking time do not worry as the soufflés will not collapse.) Serve immediately.

Serves 4-6

GRUYÈRE AND WATERCRESS ROULADE

Having worked for many years for 'Cheeses from Switzerland', I've learnt how versatile Swiss cheese can be. It is always a good idea to use top quality cheeses in cooking for their intensity of flavour and the texture of the finished dish. Roulades such as this one are so easy to make. Cooked in the Aga they are always moist and therefore easy to roll. I would highly recommend using Bake-O-Glide to line the tin and to help roll up the roulade when it is filled. Alternatively use baking parchment.

175g/6oz Gruyère cheese, grated
50g/2oz soft curd cheese
5 eggs, separated
150ml/5fl oz single cream
50g/2oz Parmesan cheese, grated
pepper

Filling
250ml/9fl oz crème fraîche
85g-bag prepared watercress or a large bunch watercress trimmed and
washed
salt and pepper

Line the large roasting tin with a sheet of Bake-O-Glide.

Place the Gruyère, curd cheese, egg yolks and single cream in a bowl and mix well. Season only with pepper not salt, as Gruyère is salty when cooked.

Whisk the egg whites to soft peaks. Beat 1 tablespoon of egg white into the cheese mixture and then fold in the remaining egg white, until just mixed. Pour into the lined roasting tin and gently spread it to the edges. Hang the tin on the bottom set of runners of the roasting oven for 12-15 minutes, until the roulade is set and a pale golden. Remove from the oven and scatter over the Parmesan cheese. Allow the roulade to go cold in the tin.

Lay a plain sheet of Bake-O-Glide on the worktop and tip out the roulade, Parmesan side down. Peel off the tin lining sheet. Spread the roulade with the crème fraîche, right to the edges, and then cover with the watercress, removing any tough stalks. Season with salt and pepper.

Starting with a long edge roll up like a Swiss roll, using the Bake-O-Glide to help you. Tuck the first part of the roll under well and then the rolling should be easy. Chill to set the shape then slice into portions with a sharp knife.

Serves 6 as a main course

OUEFS EN COCOTTE

This is a traditional French dish, a lovely way to cook eggs for supper. To further enhance the flavour you may like to infuse the warmed cream with some herbs or garlic. Just leave to stand for half an hour, strain and use.

8 eggs
butter
salt and pepper
150ml/¼ pint double cream

Butter the sides and bases of 8 ramekin dishes or small cups.

Carefully crack an egg into each one and season with salt and pepper. Spoon a tablespoon of cream over each egg.

Stand the ramekin dishes in a roasting tin and fill the tin with enough hot water to come half way up the sides of the ramekin dishes.

For a two-oven Aga hang the tin on the bottom set of runners and slide the cold shelf two runners above. For a four-oven Aga hang the tin on the second set of runners from the bottom of the baking oven.

Bake for 8-10 minutes. The egg white should be set and the yolk runny.

Serves 4 for supper or 8 as a starter

SPINACH AND GOATS' CHEESE QUESADILLAS WITH FRESH TOMATO SALSA

These Mexican filled tortillas can be quickly made using store-cupboard ingredients providing you have spinach either in the freezer or, for preference, fresh from the garden. Homemade tortillas are best if you have the time to make them. You can, of course, use a range of ingredients for the filling. Serve with a fresh tangy tomato salsa and some creamy cool thick yoghurt.

Flour Tortillas

Tortillas are traditionally made with the Mexican *masa harina* which can be expensive and difficult to find. I've used wholemeal flour as a good substitute in this recipe.

125g/4½oz wholemeal flour
3 tbsp fine cornmeal
salt
25g/1oz vegetable fat
100-125ml/3½-4fl oz lukewarm water

In a bowl mix together the flour, cornmeal and salt. Rub in the vegetable fat until really finely mixed. Make a well in the flour and stir in the water, adding enough to make a firm but not sticky dough. Wrap in cling film and leave to rest for 30 minutes.

Divide the dough into 10 portions and roll each portion on a floured worktop to a circle about 15-cm/6-inch diameter. Cover with a damp tea towel while rolling the remaining tortillas.

Brush the simmering plate with the wire brush and then lightly oil with a little vegetable oil on some kitchen paper. Place one tortilla on the prepared plate and cook for 1-2 minutes on each side, until dry on the edges and brown spots are appearing. Leave flat for quesadillas or fold for tacos.

Makes 10

Filling

3 tbsp olive oil
2 shallots, peeled and finely chopped
1 clove garlic, peeled and crushed
450g/1lb spinach, trimmed if fresh or thawed if frozen
salt and pepper
nutmeg
150g/6oz soft goats' cheese
150g/6oz Cheddar cheese, grated
1 jalapeño chilli, seeded and finely chopped
thick plain yogurt, for serving

Heat 1 tablespoon of olive oil in a saucepan and add the shallot and garlic. Cook carefully to soften but not brown. Add the spinach to the pan and cook until soft and collapsed. Season with salt and pepper and a grating of nutmeg. Tip the contents of the pan into a sieve to drain.

Lay four tortillas on a work surface, spread each one with the goats' cheese, leaving a border round the edge. Divide the spinach between the tortillas and spread over the cheese. Next add the grated cheddar and then scatter over the chopped chilli. Wet the uncovered edge with water and lay a plain tortilla on top.

Heat the remaining olive oil in a frying pan and when hot carefully fry one quesadilla until golden. Turn over and fry on the second side. Lift onto a plate and keep warm. Repeat with the remaining quesadillas.

This is enough to fill 8 tortillas. Cut into wedges and serve with thick plain yogurt and tomato salsa.

Serves 4

Fresh Tomato Salsa

2 large ripe tomatoes, cored and chopped
1 onion, peeled and chopped
1 clove garlic, peeled and chopped
1-2 jalapeño chillies, finely sliced
juice of 1 lime
1/2 tsp salt
1 tbsp chopped coriander

This goes well with Mexican and Spanish foods as it adds freshness and a little heat. The amount of chilli used is to personal taste.

Combine all the ingredients together in a mixing bowl, stir and leave to stand for at least half an hour before serving.

TOMATO AND MOZZARELLA HEARTS

This recipe was developed for a Valentine's Day cookery demonstration and later put on the Aga website. For obvious reasons this recipe serves two, but it is easy to increase the quantities for a larger group.

½ packet ready-rolled puff pastry
2 tbsp sun-dried tomato paste
½ red pepper
3 cherry tomatoes
4 slices mozzarella cheese

Unroll the pastry and cut out 2 heart shapes using a cutter, about 10cm/4 inches at the widest part. Lay on a baking tray. Spread the sun-dried tomato paste over the pastry, leaving a border around the edge. Slice the pepper into fine strips and scatter over the hearts. Slice the tomatoes and scatter over the hearts.

Cut heart shapes from the mozzarella, using a cutter slightly smaller than the pastry cutter. Lay a cheese heart on top of the pastry hearts.

Bake on the third set of runners from the top of the roasting oven for 15-20 minutes. When cooked the pastry round the edge of each heart should be risen and golden brown and the mozzarella melted.

Serves 2

AUBERGINE AND GOATS' CHEESE LAYER

These days aubergines are readily available and their wonderful flavour combines so well with goats' cheese. They have a reputation for soaking up a lot of fat, but this can be avoided if they are roasted, or blanched in boiling water before frying.

1 large aubergine, cut into 8 slices
olive oil
2 tbsp pesto
4 round slices goats' cheese
2 tomatoes, skinned, seeded and the flesh diced
salt and pepper

Heat a ridged pan on the boiling plate for 5-7 minutes. Brush the aubergine slices with olive oil on both sides. When the pan is hot 'grill' the aubergines for 3-4 minutes on either side.

Remove from the heat and spread 4 slices with pesto. Place a round of cheese on top of the pesto and the tomato pieces. Season with salt and pepper. Top with the remaining aubergine slices.

Place the sandwiches on a baking tray and carefully slide onto the third set of runners from the top of the roasting oven and cook until the cheese is bubbling.

Serve hot.

Serves 4

SOMERSET BRIE AND REDCURRANT JELLY

A quick and easy starter. The fat content can be reduced by baking this at the top of the roasting oven on a baking tray, however the crust will probably not be as crispy as the fried version.

3 tbsp redcurrant jelly
175g/6oz Somerset brie, still firm and not runny
1 egg, beaten
75g/3oz fresh breadcrumbs
vegetable oil for frying
salad leaves to garnish

Put the redcurrant jelly in a basin and stand on the back of the Aga to soften.

Cut the cheese into 4 even portions. Pour the beaten egg onto a plate and put the breadcrumbs onto a plate. Dip the cheese portions in the egg and then the breadcrumbs.

Heat the oil in a roomy frying pan and fry the cheese portions on each side until crisp, but take care not to allow the cheese to ooze out. Remove from the pan and drain on absorbent kitchen paper.

Place the cheese on a plate and spoon on some of the softened redcurrant jelly. Add the salad leaves to garnish.

Serves 4

JACKET POTATOES TOPPED WITH SALSA MEXICANA

These are so often the first food cooked in a new Aga! Of course once you have jacket potatoes from the Aga no others will do. Some people like to rub oil and salt into the skin of their potatoes.

1 potato per person, scrubbed

Cut a cross through the skin on one side of the potato. Place on the shelf of the roasting oven, wherever it happens to be. The potato will take between 1 and 1½ hours. It's cooked when the outside is crispy and the inside soft.

Do not keep warm in the simmering oven as the skin will go soft. It is best to remove from the oven if the potato is cooked and you are not quite ready to eat it. Pop the potatoes back in the roasting oven to heat up just before serving. When cooked squeeze the underside of the potato to open up the cross cut and add your chosen topping.

Salsa Mexicana

2 large ripe tomatoes, cored and chopped
1 onion, peeled and diced
1 clove garlic, peeled and crushed
2 jalapeño chillies, finely sliced
juice of 1 lime
½ tsp salt
1 tbsp chopped coriander
1 tbsp water

This is a refreshing salsa to accompany Mexican food. Also excellent as a topping for jacket potatoes as here.

Combine all the ingredients together in a bowl and mix well. Cover and leave to stand for 30 minutes before serving.

Some Alternative Fillings

•Butter
•Grated hard cheese such as Double Gloucester, Gruyère
•Tomato salsa
•Soured cream with chopped chives
•Crispy fried onions

MAIN COURSES

CRESPOLINE

A dish traditionally made using cannelloni which are not easy to find. If that's the case use the mixture to fill a lasagne dish.

225g/8oz spinach leaves
175g/6oz ricotta
freshly grated nutmeg
salt and pepper
8 cannelloni tubes
300ml/10fl oz passata

Sauce
40g/1½ oz butter
40g/1½ oz flour
450ml/15fl oz milk
50g/2oz butter

Wash the spinach leaves and place in a saucepan and cover with a lid. Cook on the simmering plate with just the water that is clinging to the leaves, until the spinach has wilted. Drain off any excess moisture and roughly chop.

To make the sauce, put the milk, butter and flour into a saucepan and whisk constantly over a medium heat until the sauce has thickened and is smooth and glossy. Pour the passata into a shallow oven-proof dish.

In a basin mix together the chopped spinach, ricotta, a good grating of nutmeg and salt and pepper. Use this mixture to fill the cannelloni tubes. Lay each filled tube on top of the tomato passata. Pour over the sauce and sprinkle over the grated Parmesan.

At this stage the pasta will be best if left to stand for 30 minutes before baking, if time allows.

To bake in a two-oven Aga hang the shelf on the bottom set of runners of the roasting oven, slide in the crespoline dish and bake for 25-30 minutes, until golden brown and piping hot.

To bake in the four-oven Aga put the oven shelf on the bottom set of runners of the baking oven, put in the crespoline dish and bake for 30-40 minutes, until golden brown and piping hot.

Serves 4

SPAGHETTI WITH ONION SAUCE

Onions cook so well in the simmering oven. It is important to cook then slowly before caramelising to get the best flavour from them. This unusual recipe can be made in advance, but add the chopped parsley at the last minute to give a fresh flavour and colour.

700g/1½lb onions, peeled and thinly sliced
2 tbsp olive oil
25g/1oz butter
100ml/4fl oz dry white wine
2 tbsp parsley, chopped
Parmesan or Parmigiano-Reggiano, grated
500-700g/1lb2oz spaghetti, fresh or dried
salt and pepper

Heat the oil and butter in a roomy shallow pan. Add the onions to the pan and toss in the hot fat. When hot and bubbling, cover with a lid and transfer to the simmering oven for 1-1½ hours, until the onions are really soft.

When the onions are cooked return the pan to the simmering plate and remove the lid. Bubble the mixture until all the onion juices have evaporated and continue to cook until the onions are turning a pale golden. Watch! They can easily burn!

When the onions are a golden brown add the wine and a good seasoning of salt and pepper. Bubble until most of the wine has evaporated.

Stir in the chopped parsley just before serving with the cooked spaghetti and hand round the grated cheese to scatter over.

Serves 4

PASTA WITH ASPARAGUS AND PARMESAN

A very quick and easy supper dish to serve in the spring when asparagus is in season. I know that asparagus is in the supermarkets all the year round but it just doesn't have the same flavour after it's travelled half way round the world.

400g/14oz asparagus
400g/14oz dried pasta shapes, e.g. penne or spirals
25g/1oz butter
1 onion, peeled and finely chopped
90ml/3fl oz white wine
300ml/1/2 pint double cream
50g/2oz Parmesan, grated
salt and pepper

Cut the asparagus into 5-cm/2-inch lengths. Bring a small pan of water to the boil and blanch the asparagus for 3-4 minutes, or until tender. Drain the asparagus, reserving the liquid.

Bring a large pan of salted water to the boil on the boiling plate and cook the pasta, according to the packet guidelines, until al dente. Drain.

Meanwhile prepare the sauce. Melt the butter in a saucepan and sauté the onion until soft but not browning. Add the asparagus, the wine and 5 tablespoons of the reserved cooking liquid. Bubble well to reduce the liquid and enhance the flavours. Add the cream and stir well while heating gently until the sauce just starts to bubble. Stir in half the Parmesan and then adjust the seasoning.

Pour the sauce over the pasta and toss well.

Serves 4

FETA AND ROAST VEGETABLE PASTA

I find this is a fairly quick and easy dish to prepare. I have specified riccioli because its rounded shape catches the sauce, however any similar fresh or dried pasta can be used. I like to keep a 300g-jar of feta in Provençal oil and herbs in the fridge and find this works well in this dish. Substitute the olive oil in the recipe for the oil in the jar.

1 red pepper
1 yellow pepper
1 aubergine
1 courgette
2 cloves garlic, peeled
1 red onion, peeled and quartered
salt and pepper
2 tbsp olive oil
200g/7oz feta cheese cut into small cubes
sprig thyme
400g/14oz-can chopped tomatoes
2 tbsp tomato purée
50g/2oz pitted black olives
500g/1lb 2oz riccioli pasta, cooked and drained

De-seed the peppers and cut into strips. Top and tail the aubergine and courgettes and cut into slices. Place all the vegetables on a baking tray with the garlic and onion. Dribble over the oil and season.

Hang on the top set of runners of the roasting oven and roast the vegetables for 15-20 minutes, until softening and charring round the edge. Pour over the can of tomatoes and stir in the tomato purée. Return to the oven for a further 5 minutes. Remove from the oven and stir in the olives and the feta cubes. Toss the roast vegetable mixture into cooked pasta and serve immediately.

Serves 4

PASTA AND MUSHROOM WITH TWO CHEESES

A quick and simple supper dish.

250g/9oz ribbon noodles
25g/1oz butter
1 clove garlic, peeled and crushed
250g/9oz mushrooms, finely sliced
50g/2oz blue Stilton
60ml/4 tbsp double cream
salt and pepper
1 egg, beaten
100g/3½oz mozzarella cheese, grated

Cook the noodles in boiling, salted water until just tender. Follow cooking times on the packet as different varieties can vary. Drain well.

Melt the butter in a large frying pan and cook the mushrooms and garlic until just softening. Crumble in the Stilton, stir for 1-2 minutes and then stir in the cream. Season with pepper.

Return the cooked pasta to the saucepan and pour over the sauce and the beaten egg. Toss well to coat the pasta with the sauce. Tip into a well buttered ovenproof dish. Sprinkle over the grated mozzarella cheese.

For the two-oven Aga place the shelf on the floor of the roasting oven or for the four-oven Aga place the shelf on the third set of runners from the top of the baking oven. Put in the dish of pasta and bake for 10-15 minutes (allow longer if the dish has been made in advance and is chilled), until bubbling and golden brown.

Serves 4

MACARONI AND BROCCOLI CHEESE

This is a slight variation on an old favourite which I will remember making for my O-level cookery exam! I have used Red Leicester cheese here, but you can experiment with any of the English cheeses.

225g/8oz broccoli florets
salt and pepper
175g/6oz macaroni or other pasta shape
600ml/1 pint milk
50g/2oz plain flour
50g/2oz butter
1 tsp mustard
175g/6oz Red Leicester cheese

Wash the broccoli and cook in boiling, salted water until just tender. Drain well and put into a shallow ovenproof dish.

Bring a large pan of salted water to the boil and pour in the pasta. Return to the boil and cook either on the boiling plate or on the floor of the roasting oven until cooked. You will need to look at the guidelines on the packet as dried pasta varies. Drain well. Return to the pan.

Place the milk, flour, butter, a seasoning of salt and pepper and the mustard in a saucepan. Stand on the simmering plate and whisk constantly to make a glossy smooth sauce. The sauce will have thickened, it should be the consistency of single cream. Remove from the heat and stir in three-quarters of the grated cheese.

Stir the sauce into the pasta and then pour over the broccoli. Sprinkle the remaining cheese on the top. Put the shelf on the third set of runners from the top of the roasting oven and slide in the macaroni dish. Bake for 15-20 minutes until golden brown and piping hot.

Serves 4

ONION TART

One of the great things about the Aga is that the whole of the oven can be used as there is no single source of heat. This means that the floor of the roasting oven is a really useful cooking surface. In the case of this onion tart recipe and other pastry dishes no pre-baking is necessary to achieve a crisp pastry finish.

4 medium red or white onions, peeled
1 tbsp olive oil
salt and pepper
500g shortcrust pastry
3 eggs
125ml/1/4 pint single cream
125ml/1/4 pint milk

Cut each onion into eight portions. Lay them on a small baking tray and dribble over the olive oil. Hang the tray on the top set of runners of the roasting oven and roast the onions until soft and just colouring round the edges, about 20 minutes. Allow to cool.

Line a shallow 23-cm/9-inch flan dish with the shortcrust pastry. Beat together the eggs, milk and cream and season with salt and pepper. Lay the cooled roast onions in the pastry case and pour on the egg custard mixture. Slide the flan dish onto the floor of the roasting oven and bake for 20-30 minutes until the pastry is a crisp golden brown and the filling is set.

Serve with a salad of freshly picked leaves dressed with good walnut oil and your best red wine vinegar.

Serves 6-8

VEGETARIAN TART

I keep puff pastry in the freezer as a useful standby for recipes like this. Add any fillings you like. Here the vegetables are roasted which brings out their flavour, and ricotta cheese adds body.

3 red peppers, quartered and seeded
1 medium aubergine, halved and sliced
1 red onion, peeled and quartered
1 tbsp olive oil
225g/8oz mushrooms, finely sliced
50g/2oz butter
150ml/¼ pint double cream
450g/1lb spinach
grated nutmeg
425g-pack ready-rolled puff pastry
225g/8oz ricotta
salt and pepper
1 egg, beaten

Place the peppers, aubergine and red onion on a baking tray and dribble over the olive oil. Place on the top set of runners of the roasting oven and roast for 20-25 minutes, until softening and just colouring. Set aside to cool.

Melt half the butter (25g/1oz) in a saucepan and sauté the mushrooms until soft but not browning. Allow the juices to bubble and evaporate and then add the cream. Continue to bubble well until the mushrooms are coated in the creamy sauce. Set aside to cool.

In a roomy saucepan, melt the remaining butter (25g/1oz), add the spinach, and toss around in the melted butter. Cook until wilted and then drain off any liquid. Roughly chop and season with nutmeg. Set aside to cool.

Lay the pastry on a long baking tray (this roll of pastry fits perfectly on the large Aga baking tray that slides on the runners). Spread the

ricotta down the middle of the pastry sheet, season with salt and pepper. Lay the roast vegetables on top, follow with a layer of spinach and finish with a layer of the mushrooms. Season well.

Cut diagonal slashes in the pastry on either side of the filling. Brush the pastry edges with beaten egg and then overlap the pastry strips alternating side to side, like a plait. Brush with beaten egg.

Bake on the third set of runners from the top of the roasting oven for 15 minutes and then transfer to the floor of the roasting oven for a further 10 minutes to crisp the base. Serve when the pastry is puffed and golden brown.

Serve hot.

Serves 8-10

CHEESE AND ASPARAGUS TART

The cheese pastry adds a crispness to the case that contrasts superbly with the delicately flavoured filling. Any asparagus trimmings can be used for soup (see page 32).

Pastry
175g/6oz plain flour
75g/3oz butter, cut into small chunks
75g/3oz Cheddar cheese, finely grated
1 tsp mustard
salt and pepper

Filling
450g/1lb asparagus, trimmed
3 large eggs
450ml/³/₄ pint single cream
salt and pepper
grated nutmeg

To prepare the pastry, place the flour in a bowl and add the butter. Rub the butter in until the mixture resembles breadcrumbs. Alternatively, this may be done with a mixer or a food processor. Next, stir in the grated cheese, mustard and a seasoning of salt and pepper. Bind the mixture together with enough cold water to make a firm but not dry dough. Knead lightly and then roll out to fit a 22-cm/9-inch flan dish. Chill well.

Prepare the asparagus. Either steam it or cook until just tender in a little boiling water. Drain and cool.

Beat together the eggs and cream and season with salt and pepper.

Lay the asparagus in the pastry case. Pour over the egg mixture and grate over a little nutmeg.

Place the tart on the floor of the roasting oven and slide the cold shelf two runners from the bottom of the oven. Bake until the pastry is a pale golden colour and the filling is set, usually about 20 minutes.

Serve warm or cold.

Serves 6

LEEK TART

This tart has a yeast-based case rather than pastry, easy to make and a bit different. If you can't get fresh yeast use a sachet of easy-blend yeast – though the flavour may not be quite as good, it is a useful standby.

250g/9oz strong flour
1 tsp salt
50g/2oz butter, softened but not oily
15g/1/2 oz yeast
150ml/1/4 pint milk, warmed
2 eggs, beaten

Filling
50g/2oz butter
1kg/2lb leeks, trimmed, sliced and well washed
salt and pepper
150ml/1/4 pint crème fraîche
1 egg
1 egg yolk

Mix the flour and salt together in a large mixing bowl and rub in the butter. In a separate basin, cream together the yeast and warm milk. Pour into the flour along with the beaten eggs. Mix well to form a dough, it will be sticky at this stage. Knead well on a very lightly floured worktop, for 5 minutes to make a smooth, pliable dough. Return to the mixing bowl and cover with a damp tea towel or oiled cling film. Stand on a trivet or chef's pad on the back of the Aga until doubled in size.

Meanwhile prepare the filling. Melt the butter in a large pan and sauté the leeks for 2-3 minutes. Season with salt and pepper. Stir well and cover with a tight fitting lid and transfer to the simmering oven for 30 minutes, until the leeks are soft.

Turn the risen dough onto a lightly floured surface and roll out to fit a 23-cm/9-inch buttered pie tin or deep flan tin. Line the tin with the dough.

Beat together the crème fraîche, egg and egg yolk and a seasoning of salt and pepper. Spoon the cooked leeks into the dough case and pour over the crème fraîche mixture.

Leave the tart on a trivet or chef's pad on top of the simmering plate lid until the dough crust is puffy, about 10-15 minutes.

Bake on the floor of the roasting oven for 15 minutes and then move up to the shelf on the third set of runners from the top of the oven for a further 10-15 minutes, until the filling is set and the crust is golden brown.

Serve hot.

Serves 6-8

PARSNIP AND BLUE CHEESE TART

This is one of my favourite Christmas-time recipes that I often make for my Aga cookery demonstrations. Over the years I have converted many people to parsnips and blue cheese.

350g/12oz shortcrust pastry
225g/8oz parsnips
3 eggs
300ml/$\frac{1}{2}$ pint single cream
100g/4oz blue Stilton or other blue cheese
nutmeg, pinch grated
pepper

Roll out the pastry to fit a 23-cm/9-inch flan tin or dish. Chill.

Peel the parsnips and cut into medium sized dice. Place in a saucepan with about 2.5cm/1 inch of water. Cover and boil for 1 minute, then drain off all the water. Replace the saucepan lid and place the pan in the simmering oven for about 30 minutes, until the parsnips are soft enough to mash. Drain off any excess moisture and then mash the parsnips with a fork. Set aside to cool.

Beat together the eggs and the cream, crumble in the Stilton and season with the nutmeg and the pepper.

Spread the cooled parsnips in the pastry case and pour on the egg and cheese mixture. At this stage the mixture looks horrible! I promise it tastes better than it looks at this stage! Slide the tart onto the floor of the roasting oven and bake for 20-25 minutes, until the pastry is golden brown and the filling is set.

Serve hot.

Serves 4

PEPPER AND WATERCRESS TART

The colours in this tart are really attractive and by using a jar of pepper strips makes it a speedy dish to prepare. The cream can be replaced with a low fat alternative, but just a spoonful makes a huge difference!

Pastry*
225g/8oz plain flour
100g/4oz butter
pinch salt
*or 500g-pack ready-made shortcrust pastry

Filling
20g/³/₄ oz butter
1 onion peeled and chopped
3 eggs
225ml/8fl oz double cream
salt and pepper
75g/3oz Cheddar cheese, grated
85g pack ready-washed watercress or a bunch washed and trimmed
290g jar mixed peppers in oil

Line a 23-cm/9-inch flan tin with the pastry.

Melt the butter in a small pan and sauté the onion until soft but not brown. Drain from the pan and scatter over the base of the pastry case.

Mix together, in a basin, the eggs, cream, a seasoning of salt and pepper and the cheese. Roughly chop the watercress, discarding any tough stalks. Scatter over the pastry case, then pour over the egg mixture. Drain the peppers and then scatter over the filling.

Bake on the floor of the roasting oven for 20-25 minutes, until golden brown and the filling is set.

Serves 6-8

ARTICHOKE AND STILTON TART

This is another Christmas recipe I developed for my cookery demonstrations in the Aga showrooms. It had to be quick and easy to make and I thought the Stilton made the dish seasonal, though any blue cheese, such as the lovely French Fourme D'Ambert, would work just as well.

450g/1lb shortcrust pastry

Filling
400g/14oz-can artichoke hearts, drained
100g/4oz Stilton cheese
3 eggs
300ml/1/2 pint single cream or cream and milk combined
pepper

Using the short crust pastry, line a 23-cm/9-inch flan dish or tin with the pastry and chill.

Cut the artichoke hearts in half and lay, cut side up, in the pastry case.

Crumble the Stilton over the pastry case.

Beat together the eggs and cream and season with pepper. Salt should not be needed as the Stilton will be salty. Pour the egg mixture over the artichokes. Place the tart on the floor of the roasting oven for 20-25 minutes, until the filling is set, the pastry is crisp and golden and the tart a pale golden.

Serves 6-8

TOMATO AND CHEESE CLAFOUTI

A clafouti is usually thought of as a sweet fruit-filled batter. In this recipe I have combined the sweetness of the cherry tomatoes with a savoury filling.

300g/11oz cherry tomatoes
1 tbsp plain flour
2 eggs
4 tbsp crème fraîche
2 tbsp milk
2 tbsp snipped chives
60g/2oz Parmesan cheese, grated
salt and pepper

Butter a shallow ovenproof dish, about 1.5-litre/2¾-pint capacity.

Cut the tomatoes in half and lay cut side down over the base of the dish.

Place the flour in a mixing bowl and whisk in the eggs, milk and crème fraîche to make a smooth batter. Season with salt and pepper and stir in half the grated Parmesan cheese and the chopped chives.

Pour the batter over the tomatoes and sprinkle over the remaining Parmesan cheese.

Place the shelf on the bottom set of runners of the roasting oven and slide in the clafouti dish. Bake for 20-25 minutes until puffed and risen and golden brown.

Serve warm.

Serves 4

TOMATO AND OLIVE FLAN

This is a wonderful store-cupboard flan to bring a flavour of summer eating onto your table!

Pastry
175g/6oz plain flour
75g/3oz butter, cut into small chunks
25g/1oz Parmesan cheese, grated
pinch of salt
pinch of mustard powder

Filling
3 eggs
200ml/7fl oz crème fraîche
150ml/¼ pint milk
8-10 black olives, pitted and halved lengthways
4-6 sun-dried tomatoes, cut into strips
25g/1oz Parmesan cheese, grated

To make the pastry: firstly, sift the flour into a mixing bowl and then add the butter, which should be at room temperature and cut into small chunks. Rub in the butter until the mixture resembles fine breadcrumbs. Stir in the Parmesan cheese, a pinch of salt and a pinch of mustard powder, if you have some. Add enough cold water, about 5 tablespoons, to make a firm, but not dry dough. Roll it out to fit a 23-cm/9-inch flan tin. Chill well.

Beat together the eggs, crème fraîche, milk and a grinding of pepper. Lay the olives and the sun-dried tomatoes in the base of the pastry case. Pour over the egg mixture and sprinkle over the Parmesan cheese. To bake: slide the flan tin on the floor of the roasting oven and bake for 20-25 minutes, or until the filling is set and lightly golden brown. Serve warm.

Serves 6

ROAST SUMMER VEGETABLE FLAN

Although I call this 'summer vegetable' these vegetables seem to be available all year round. It's another dish that includes those wonderful Aga roasted vegetables. If you end up roasting too many for your flan dish, they are very good kept in the fridge and eaten later.

350g/12oz shortcrust pastry

Filling
1 red pepper, seeded
1 medium aubergine, trimmed
1 small red onion, peeled
1 courgette, trimmed
1 tbsp olive oil
salt and pepper
3 eggs
300ml/¹/₂ pint single cream, or cream and milk
2-3 tbsp grated Parmesan, optional

Line a 23-cm/9-inch flan tin with the shortcrust pastry and chill.

Cut the vegetables into even sized chunks, about 2.5-cm/1-inch square. Line the shallow baking tray with Bake-O-Glide and put on the vegetables. Drizzle over the oil and add a grinding of salt. Slide the tin onto the second set of runners from the top of the roasting oven and roast for 20-25 minutes, until the vegetables are just colouring and just cooked. Remove from the oven and allow to cool.

Beat together the eggs and cream and season with salt and pepper. Spoon the vegetables into the pastry case and pour over the egg mixture. Sprinkle on the cheese if using. To bake: slide the flan onto the floor of the roasting oven for 20-25 minutes, until the pastry is golden brown and the filling is set.

Serves 6

WHITE STILTON TORTE WITH ROAST VEGETABLES

I have used white Stilton, a neglected cheese beside its big blue brother. It has a creaminess that isn't always noticeable in blue Stilton. If you can't find white Stilton, then substitute Wensleydale or Caerphilly.

Base
175g/6oz Caerphilly cheese, crumbled
75g/3oz butter, softened
175g/6oz self-raising flour
1 tbsp mustard, smooth for preference
3 eggs, beaten
60ml/4oz tbsp boiling water
150g/5oz white Stilton, crumbled
1 tbsp sesame seeds

Topping
Selection of vegetables, e.g. carrots, peppers, red onions
6 cherry tomatoes
olive oil
salt

Prepare the vegetables for roasting: peel the carrots and cut into thick slices, de-seed and cut the peppers into chunky pieces and finally peel and quarter the onions. Place on a shallow roasting tray. Drizzle with 2-3 tablespoons of olive oil and season with salt. Set aside.

Butter a deep 19-cm/7½-inch cake or flan tin.

Mix together the Caerphilly and the butter. Add the flour, mustard and eggs and stir in. Add the boiling water and gently stir in to make a smooth mixture. Spoon half the mixture into the base of the buttered tin. Level off. Cover with the crumbled white Stilton and then spread the remaining mixture on top. Sprinkle over the sesame seeds.

Hang the baking tray of vegetables on the second set of runners, from the top of the roasting oven.

Place the oven shelf on the bottom set of runners of the roasting oven and put in the tin with the torte mixture, taking care not to put under the roast vegetable tin as it will mask the heat.

Bake for 30-35 minutes until golden brown and firm to the touch. Remove from the tin and top with the roast vegetables and the cherry tomato halves.

Serve hot.

Serves 4

ROAST VEGETABLE TATIN

This is a slightly different way of using root vegetables to make a main course – and the Aga is just so versatile when it comes to cooking tatins. But do be careful not to leave the tatin in the pan it's been cooked in because the caramel will set and you will find it really hard to serve.

175g/6oz celeriac, peeled and sliced
175g/6oz sweet potatoes, peeled and sliced
175g/6oz carrots, peeled and sliced
175g/6oz shallots, peeled and sliced
100g/4oz leeks, trimmed and sliced
2 tbsp olive oil
salt and pepper
1 tsp fennel seeds and 1 tsp coriander seeds, ground
25g/1oz butter
2 tsp sugar
75g/3oz ready-to-eat apricots, quartered
225g/8oz shortcrust or puff pastry

Place the celeriac, sweet potatoes, carrots, shallots and leeks on a roasting tray. Drizzle over the oil and season with salt and pepper. Hang the tin on the second set of runners of the roasting oven and cook the vegetables for 30 minutes, toss and stir well, adding the spices and cook for another 10 minutes.

Place the butter in an ovenproof frying pan or pie tin about 28-cm/ 11-inch diameter. Place on the floor of the roasting oven for a few minutes until the butter has melted. Sprinkle over the sugar.

Mix the apricots with the vegetables and lay the vegetables in an even layer on the base of the frying pan or tin.

Roll the pastry to fit the tin or pan. Lay the pastry on top of the vegetables and lightly press down around the edges.

Place the tin or frying pan on the floor of the roasting oven and bake for 15-20 minutes, until the pastry is golden brown all over. Allow to cool for 4 or 5 minutes and then invert onto a serving plate.

Serves 4

ONION TATIN

By slowly cooking the onions in the simmering oven they become wonderfully sweet. You can also use red onions for this tatin, it's up to you.

4 large onions, peeled and finely sliced
2 tbsp olive oil
25g/1oz butter
thyme, a few fresh sprigs
225g/8oz shortcrust pastry

Heat the oil in a large, shallow saucepan or casserole dish. Stir in the onions and sweat in the hot oil for 1-2 minutes, stirring well. Cover with a lid and transfer to the simmering oven for 50-60 minutes, until the onions are really soft but not coloured.

Place the butter in a shallow pie or cake tin, approximately 23-cm/ 9-inch diameter. Place on the warming plate or on a warm spot on top of the Aga until the butter melts. Sprinkle over the thyme. Spread the cooked onions over the thyme.

Roll out the pastry to fit the dish. Place over the onions. Trim the pastry. Place the dish directly on the floor of the roasting oven and bake for about 20 minutes, until the pastry is golden brown.

Remove from the oven, leave to set for 2-3 minutes and then invert onto a serving plate so that the caramelised onions are on the top.

Serves 4-6

CAULIFLOWER AND POTATO CURRY

3 tbsp vegetable oil
1 onion, peeled and chopped
2 tsp coriander seeds
$1/_2$ tsp mustard seeds
$1/_2$ tsp fenugreek seeds
$1/_2$ tsp cumin seeds
1 red chilli, dried, to taste
400ml-can coconut milk
1-cm/$1/_2$-inch piece ginger, peeled and chopped
4 cloves garlic, peeled and chopped
2.5-cm/$1 1/_2$-inch piece cinnamon stick
4 peppercorns
2 cloves
$1/_2$ tsp turmeric
$1/_2$ tsp paprika

700g/$1 1/_2$lb potatoes, peeled and cut into large cube
1 head cauliflower, broken into florets
salt to taste

Heat 1 tablespoon of oil in a large shallow saucepan. Add the chopped onion to the pan and cook until softening. Stir in the coriander seeds, mustard seeds, fenugreek seeds, cumin seeds and crushed dried chilli.

Stir well and fry for 2-3 minutes until the seeds begin to pop and release their intoxicating aromas. Tip the pan contents into a blender along with half the can of coconut milk. Blend well and strain through a sieve.

Heat the remaining 2 tablespoons of oil in the pan and add the garlic and ginger, taking care not to burn. Add the cinnamon stick, peppercorns, cloves, turmeric and paprika. Stir well and add the potato, the spicy coconut mixture and the remaining coconut milk.

Fill the can half full with water, rinse around and add to the potato mixture.

Cover and simmer for 10 minutes and then stir in the cauliflower. Season with salt, cover the pan and simmer for a further 10-15 minutes, until the cauliflower is just cooked. Check the seasoning.

Serve with rice, such as Basmati.

Serves 4

MIXED VEGETABLE CURRY

There are many, many recipes for vegetable curry – this is one I particularly like.

4 tbsp vegetable oil
75g/3oz desiccated coconut
1 red chilli, seeded and finely sliced
1 tbsp coriander seeds
4 cloves
10 peppercorns
1 x 5-cm/2-inch stick cinnamon
1 onion, peeled and sliced
1/2 tsp mustard seeds
1/2 tsp cumin seeds
1/4 tsp turmeric
1 bay leaf
1 onion, peeled and chopped
1 blade mace
1kg/21/4 lb mixed vegetables, e.g. sweet potato, carrot, turnip,
carrot, peas
squeeze of lemon or lime juice

Heat 1 tablespoon of the oil in a frying pan and cook the coconut for 2-3 minutes. Set aside in a bowl.

Put the chillies and coriander seeds in the pan and cook for 3 minutes before adding the cloves, peppercorns and cinnamon stick. Put the coconut, roast spices, sliced onion and 300ml/1/2 pint of water in a blender and blend well.

In an oven and flameproof pan or casserole dish heat the remaining oil. Add the mustard seeds, cumin and turmeric powder, stir and cook for 1 minute before adding the bay leaf and chopped onion. Fry until the onion is browning and then add the coconut mixture and the mace. Cook for 1-2 minutes and then add the vegetables, peeled and cut into medium dice (if using beans or peas add these

10 minutes before the end of cooking).

Add 300ml/½ pint of water and a seasoning of salt. Bring to the boil, cover and put in the simmering oven for 1 hour, until the vegetables are cooked but still holding their shape. If the sauce remains thin allow the sauce to bubble on the simmering plate for a few minutes. Some vegetables absorb and thicken the sauce more than others.

Add a squeeze of lemon or lime juice to taste just before serving.

Serves 4-6

FRUIT AND NUT CURRY

This is a famous recipe served as part of a buffet lunch at the Taj Mahal hotel in Bombay. The quantities of nuts may not seem large but I assure you this is a very satisfying dish!

100g/4oz dried apricots, soaked in warm water
for at least 1 hour
100g/4oz almonds, blanched
75g/3oz pistachio nuts
100g/4oz cashew nuts
250g/9oz Greek-style plain yogurt
salt and pepper
1 tbsp vegetable oil
1 bay leaf
1 x 5-cm/2-inch stick cinnamon
4 cloves
4 green cardamoms
3 onions, peeled and finely chopped
2.5-cm/1-inch piece fresh ginger
4 cloves garlic, peeled and crushed
3 green chillies, seeded and finely shredded
1 tsp ground coriander
1/2 tsp ground cumin
1 tsp red chilli powder
2 tomatoes, chopped
1 1/2 tbsp ghee or clarified butter
50g/2oz walnut halves
100g/4oz plump seedless raisins
1 tsp garam masala
3 tbsp single cream
6 cherries, maraschino if you can get them or else glacé
cherries soaked in warm water to remove their stickiness

Soak the apricots in water for 1 1/2 hours. Soak the almonds and pistachios in enough hot water to cover, for 1 hour, then drain and reserve the liquid. Skin the almonds. Place half the cashew nuts into a blender with a little water and grind to form a paste. Whisk the

yoghurt with a seasoning of salt and pepper, this will make the yoghurt smoother for mixing in at the end.

Heat the oil in a large frying pan and add the bay leaf, cinnamon, cloves and cardamoms. Add the onions and fry gently until the onions are just starting to colour. Fry gently to avoid burning the spices. Add the ginger, garlic and chillies and sauté for 5-10 minutes, by this time the onions should be quite dark.

Add the ground coriander, cumin and red chilli powder to the pan and stir well. Sauté for 3-4 minutes. Add the tomatoes and cook for a further 5 minutes.

Remove the pan from the heat and discard the bay leaf. Pour the contents of the pan into a blender and purée, and then pour back into the pan. Next add the yoghurt, cashew nut paste and 150ml/5 fl oz water. Stir well and bring to a bubble on the simmering plate. Cover with a lid and transfer to the simmering oven for half an hour.

While the sauce is cooking in the simmering oven heat the ghee in a frying pan and sauté the almonds, cashews, walnuts, raisins, apricots and most of the cashews for 5-6 minutes.

Remove the sauce from the simmering oven and add the sautéd fruit and nuts. Return the pan to the simmering oven for about 20 minutes. Stir in the garam masala, cook for a further 5 minutes and then serve, garnished with swirls of cream, pistachios and maraschino cherries.

Serve with rice or naan bread.

Serves 4, or more as part of a curry selection

Naan Bread

350g/12oz self-raising flour
salt
3 tsp ground cumin
500g/1lb 2oz Greek-style yogurt

This is a cheat's way of making fresh naans. I cannot find the original recipe so this guessing seems to work well!

Place the flour in a mixing bowl along with the cumin and a good seasoning of salt. Add the yogurt to make a slightly sticky dough. Knead lightly and then cover with a tea towel or cling film for an hour.

Knead the dough on a lightly floured work top. Divide the dough into 12 pieces and roll to a round.

Lightly oil the simmering plate and put on four naan breads. Cook until browning and puffed. Turn over and cook the other side. Keep warm wrapped in a napkin in the simmering oven. Continue to cook the remaining naan breads.

Makes 12 individual breads

CAULIFLOWER AND POTATO BAKE

A variation on the good old cauliflower cheese! This can be prepared in advance and baked at the last minute, making for a really useful instant supper dish.

450g/1lb potatoes, peeled and thinly sliced
1 small cauliflower, broken into florets
1 clove garlic
salt and pepper
150ml/¹/₄ pint single cream
fresh nutmeg
50g/2oz Cheddar cheese, grated

Half fill a large pan with salted water and bring to the boil. Plunge in the potato slices and the cauliflower florets. Boil for 4-5 minutes, until the potatoes and cauliflower are just softening. Drain well.

Cut the clove of garlic in half and rub it around a shallow 1.2l/2-pint ovenproof dish. Then butter the dish well. Layer in the potatoes and cauliflower. Season the cream with salt and pepper and a grating of nutmeg and pour over the potatoes and cauliflower base. Finally sprinkle with the grated cheese.

For a two-oven Aga: put the shelf on the floor of the roasting oven. Slide in the dish and bake for 30-40 minutes. For the four-oven Aga: put the shelf on the second set of runners from the bottom. Slide in the dish and bake for 40-50 minutes. Cook until the vegetables are firm but cooked when prodded with a sharp knife and the topping is golden brown.

Serves 4-6

VEGETABLE HOT POT

A handy dish that can be left cooking slowly in the simmering oven while you are gardening or collecting the children from school. The range of vegetables can vary according to season or what's available locally.

50g/2oz butter
1 clove garlic, cut in half
2 onions, peeled and sliced
4 carrots, peeled and sliced
1 small swede, peeled and diced
2 parsnips, peeled and sliced
4 Jerusalem artichokes, scrubbed and sliced
1/2 head of celeriac, peeled and diced
2 leeks, trimmed, washed and sliced
a bunch parsley and thyme, tied with string
450g/1lb potatoes, scrubbed and sliced thinly
300ml/1/2 pint vegetable stock
1 tbsp flour, seasoned with salt and pepper

Rub the inside of a 2l/3-4 pint casserole dish with the cut edges of the clove of garlic, then butter the inside of the dish.

Put the seasoned flour and one type of prepared vegetable into a large plastic bag and give it a gentle shake. Lay the floured vegetables in the prepared casserole dish in layers. Do not flour the potatoes.

When all the vegetables except the potatoes have been layered up bury the bunch of herbs in the middle of the dish. Then lay the thinly sliced potatoes attractively on top. Pour over the vegetable stock and cover with a lid.

Place the casserole on the floor of the roasting oven for 20-30 minutes or until piping hot. Then move it to the simmering oven for 1½-2 hours, until the vegetables are tender when tested with the point of a knife.

Remove the lid of the casserole and return it to the roasting oven. With the shelf on the second set of runners from the bottom of the oven. (This position will depend on the depth of your casserole dish, the dish should be as high as possible.) Cook for 20-30 minutes until the potatoes are golden brown.

Serves 4

HARICOT HOT POT

Serve with crusty bread, or equally delicious as an accompaniment.

225g/8oz dried haricot beans
2 tbsp olive oil
2 onions, peeled and sliced
4 celery sticks, sliced
2 large carrots, peeled and diced
2 parsnips, peeled and diced
300ml/¹⁄₂ pint vegetable stock
salt and pepper
2 tbsp chopped parsley
110g/4oz mushrooms, wiped and sliced

Soak the beans in plenty of cold water for several hours or overnight. Drain and place in a saucepan, cover with fresh cold water. Bring to the boil and bubble well for 10 minutes before moving to the simmering oven for 40-50 minutes, until tender but not collapsing. Drain well.

Heat the oil in a flameproof casserole dish and add the onions, celery, carrots and parsnips. Sauté until soft but not browning. Add the vegetable stock and the beans. Season with salt and pepper. Cover with a lid, bring to the boil and transfer to the simmering oven for an hour.

Stir in the mushrooms and parsley and simmer on the simmering plate for about 5 minutes until the mushrooms are cooked.

Serves 4

RUSTIC MOROCCAN STEW

The Moroccan harissa paste gives this stew a hint of chilli. If you prefer, for a hotter flavour, you can cook some whole chillies along with the vegetables.

50g/2oz dried chickpeas
50g/2oz dried haricot beans
600ml/1 pint vegetable stock
1 onion, peeled and chopped
2 carrots, peeled and sliced
2 parsnips, peeled and sliced
2 tomatoes, peeled and quartered
50g/2oz bulgar wheat or couscous
1 tbsp olive oil
1 sprig thyme
1 tsp chopped mint
2 tsp dried oregano
2 tbsp tomato purée
salt and pepper
1 tbsp harissa paste

Place the chickpeas in a basin, cover with water and soak overnight. Do the same with the haricot beans.

The next day, drain well and put the beans and chickpeas in a saucepan. Pour on the stock and bring to the boil and keep the water bubbling for 10 minutes.

Pour the beans and stock into a flameproof casserole. Add the bulgar wheat, the vegetables, chillies if using, olive oil, thyme, mint, oregano and a seasoning of salt and pepper. Cover with a lid and bring to the boil.

Once boiling move the casserole dish to the simmering oven and cook for 2 hours. Move the casserole to the simmering plate and stir in the tomato purée and the harissa paste if using. Return to a good bubble and again put the casserole back in the simmering oven for

half an hour, until the beans and vegetables are cooked but not mushy.

Remove the thyme sprig before serving and sprinkle over some chopped parsley if you have some handy.

Serve with either wholemeal bread of baked potatoes to mop up any extra juices and a small side dish of extra harissa.

Serves 6

BUTTERNUT AND CHICKPEA CASSEROLE

Squashes of all different sorts are becoming popular and of course more available in the shops. Harissa paste added at the end adds a little 'kick' to the casserole. Tabasco can be substituted for the harissa.

3 tbsp olive oil
2 onions, peeled and chopped
2 cloves garlic, peeled and crushed
1 tsp turmeric
400g/14oz-can chopped tomatoes
1 large butternut squash, peeled, seeded and cut into chunks
1 medium cauliflower, broken into florets
2 red peppers, seeded and cut into chunks
300ml/½ pint vegetable stock
400g/14oz-can chickpeas, drained
2 tsp harissa paste
1 tbsp coriander, chopped
salt and pepper

Heat the oil in a flameproof casserole. Sauté the onion until soft and then add the garlic and turmeric. Stir well in the hot pan to prevent burning. Add the tomatoes and squash, cauliflower and peppers and stir well. Add the stock and the chickpeas. Cover the dish and just bring to the boil. Transfer to the simmering oven for 1½ hours. Remove some of the juices and blend with the harissa paste. Add the chopped coriander and stir into the casserole. Heat through and adjust the seasoning.

This dish goes well with buttered couscous (see page 156).

Serves 4

LEEK AND SAFFRON RISOTTO

The secret of a creamy risotto is to slowly add the hot stock and stir constantly. If you can't get saffron risotto rice then soak a few strands of saffron in the hot stock.

25g/1oz butter
1 tbsp olive oil
500g/1lb 2oz leeks trimmed, washed and finely sliced
2 cloves garlic, peeled and crushed
225g/8oz saffron risotto rice
1 sprig rosemary
1l/1³/₄ pints vegetable stock, hot
25g/1oz flaked almonds
2 tbsp pumpkin seeds
salt and pepper

In a roomy frying pan heat the oil and the butter. Fry the leeks and the garlic for 3-4 minutes until soft but not brown. Stir in the rice and coat well with the buttery mixture. Add the sprig of rosemary. Stir in the stock, and when the rice has just about absorbed all the liquid add another ladleful. Continue like this, stirring constantly for 15 minutes or so or until the rice is cooked but still a little bite to it.

Put the almonds and the pumpkin seeds on a baking tray in the top of the roasting oven. Toast lightly.

Remove the sprig of rosemary from the risotto and adjust the seasoning. Scatter the toasted almonds and pumpkin seeds over the rice and serve immediately.

Serves 4

ASPARAGUS AND PEA RISOTTO

A wonderful spring or early summer dish with all the flavours of fresh young vegetables.

1 bunch asparagus, about 250g/8oz
175g/6oz peas, fresh or frozen
1 onion, peeled and finely chopped
2 sticks celery, finely sliced
2 tbsp olive oil
225g/8oz Arborio rice
shavings of Parmesan to serve, optional
600ml/1 pint stock

Trim the asparagus and cut each stalk into three. Put the tip ends to one side. Put the stock in a saucepan and bring to the boil. Add the remaining part of the asparagus and the fresh peas to the stock and cook for 3-4 minutes, then add the asparagus tips and, if using, the frozen peas. Cook for 2 minutes and then remove the vegetables, reserving the stock.

Heat the oil in a large frying pan and sauté the onion and celery until soft but not coloured. Add the rice and stir into the oil and onion mixture. Gradually add the hot stock, a ladle at a time, continuing to stir the rice well. This stirring will help to make a creamy risotto. Add enough stock until the rice is cooked and won't absorb any more.

Gently stir in the cooked vegetables and heat through. Serve with Parmesan shavings.

Serves 3

OVEN-ROASTED VEGETABLE MOUSSAKA

Once this dish is assembled it can be frozen before the cooking stage, which is always a help at busy times.

1 medium onion, peeled and sliced
1 sweet potato, peeled and diced
2 red peppers, seeded and roughly chopped
1 aubergine, sliced
350g/12oz potato, peeled and sliced
5 cloves garlic, peeled
5 tbsp olive oil
400g/14oz-can chopped tomatoes
4 pieces sun-dried tomatoes, snipped into strips
225g/8oz-tub cottage cheese
3 large eggs
150g/6oz grated Cheddar cheese
3 tbsp plain yogurt
salt and pepper

Line the large roasting tin with Bake-O-Glide. Put all the prepared vegetables in the lined tin. Season with salt and toss in the olive oil. Hang the tin on the top set of runners of the roasting oven and roast for 45-50 minutes, until the vegetables are cooked. Pour over the can of chopped tomatoes and the snipped sun-dried tomatoes. Mix well and return to the oven for a further 10 minutes.

In a bowl mix together the cottage cheese, eggs, Cheddar cheese and the yogurt. Season with salt and pepper.

Spoon the roast vegetables into a shallow oven-proof dish and pour over the cheese mixture. (The dish may be frozen at this stage. Thaw overnight and bake as below for 30-40 minutes.)

Bake the moussaka on the third set of runners from the top of the roasting oven for 15-20 minutes, until bubbling hot and golden brown. Alternatively if you have a four-oven Aga; cook in the baking oven with the shelf on the second set of runners from the bottom for 20-30 minutes.

Serves 3

VEGETABLE PAELLA

Paellas are traditionally thought of as being a fish or chicken dish, so this is a variation on the same theme. The vegetables can be varied to suit availability.

1 large onion, peeled and finely chopped
1 clove garlic, peeled and crushed
2 tbsp olive oil
2 large carrots, peeled and diced
1 red pepper, seeded and diced
1 green pepper, seeded and diced
1 aubergine, trimmed and cut into chunks
2 medium courgettes, trimmed and cut into chunks
450g/1 lb long grain rice
1l/1³/₄ pints vegetable stock
good pinch saffron strands, soaked in 1 tbsp hot water
sprig thyme and 1 bay leaf
110g/4oz peas, cooked if fresh, thawed if frozen
4 tomatoes, skinned and finely chopped
salt and pepper

Heat the oil in a paella dish or a large pan, one that will fit into the simmering oven. Add the onion and fry until softened but not browning. Add the garlic and the carrots. Continue to cook for 3-4 minutes, stirring often.

Then add the peppers, aubergines and courgettes. Toss the vegetables in the oil and cook for about 5 minutes.

Add the rice to the pan and stir to coat in the oil. Pour in the stock and the saffron and season with salt and pepper. Add the thyme and the bay leaf.

Cover with a lid if you have one or an old plate. Bring to the boil and transfer to the simmering oven for about 20 minutes, until the rice has cooked and the stock has been absorbed.

Remove from the oven and stir well. Remove the thyme and bay leaf and discard. Add the peas and the tomatoes and then adjust the seasoning. Serve hot.

Serves 6

SPINACH GNOCCHI

This is one of my favourite recipes from the *Four Seasons Aga Cookery Book* and uses deliciously tender leaves of freshly picked spinach. However, out of season, frozen spinach makes an excellent substitute. A further convenience, whether using fresh or frozen spinach, is that this dish can be made in advance, although I still prefer it freshly made.

450g/1lb fresh spinach, thick stalks removed & well washed
175g/6oz Ricotta cheese
50g/2oz flour
1 egg yolk
50g/2oz Gruyère cheese, grated
salt & pepper,
grated nutmeg

Sauce
15g/¹/₂oz butter
15g/¹/₂oz flour
450ml/³/₄ pint milk
50g/2oz Gruyère cheese, grated
pepper

Place the spinach in a saucepan with a lid, put on the simmering plate and cook until the spinach has wilted. Drain off any excess moisture and chop the spinach very finely or purée in a food processor or blender.

Mix the spinach with the Ricotta cheese and flour. Then beat in the egg yolk, Gruyère cheese, a little salt and pepper and a grating of nutmeg.

Dust your hands with flour and shape teaspoonfuls of mixture into little balls. Chill well.

Place a large pan of salted water on the boiling plate to boil.

Meanwhile, make the sauce: place the butter, flour and milk into a saucepan and whisk on the simmering plate until boiling and thickened. Remove from the heat and stir in the cheese and pepper. Keep warm while cooking the gnocchi.

Drop the gnocchi, one at a time, into the pan of boiling water. When they float to the surface the gnocchi are ready. Remove with a slotted spoon and place in a shallow ovenproof dish. Pour over the sauce and grate over a little nutmeg.

Serves 4

ROMAN GNOCCHI

I have made this for so many years as a store cupboard standby that I can't remember its origin. You will need to start making it several hours ahead to allow time for chilling. This is not a recipe for a low-fat diet!

300ml/½ pint milk
150g/5oz semolina
nutmeg, freshly grated
salt and pepper
75g/3oz butter
150g/5oz Parmesan grated
2 eggs, beaten

Put the milk, 300ml/½ pint water, semolina, a grating of nutmeg and the salt and bring to the boil, stirring constantly. Keep stirring and cook until the mixture is so thick that it is difficult to stir. Remove from the heat.

Beat in 25g/1oz of the butter and 75g/3oz of the Parmesan. Then add the eggs and beat in well.

Line the small roasting tin with Bake-O-Glide or buttered foil. Spread in the semolina mixture. Cover with cling film and chill well.

Butter a shallow 2l/1¾ pint ovenproof dish. Turn the semolina mixture onto a chopping board. Cut into squares approximately 5-cm/2-inch square. Lay, overlapping, in the buttered dish. Dot with the remaining butter and sprinkle over the remaining Parmesan.

Put the oven shelf on the third set of runners from the top of the roasting oven and put in the gnocchi dish. Bake for 20-25 minutes until bubbling hot and golden brown.

Serves 3-4

NUT LOAF

So many people think that vegetarian food consists of dull-looking nut loaves and rissoles! I hesitated before putting a nut loaf recipe in this book just because of this old-fashioned idea, but for nut lovers this recipe is a must. The tomato layer can be changed to blanched spinach leaves. The Cheddar cheese replaced with Danish Blue cheese.

1 tbsp olive oil
1 medium onion, peeled and finely chopped
100g/4oz fresh breadcrumbs
1 tbsp parsley, chopped
225g/8oz mixed nuts, e.g. walnuts, peanuts, cashews etc.
salt and pepper
150ml/¼ pint vegetable stock
3 medium tomatoes, sliced
50g/2oz Cheddar cheese, grated

Heat the oil in a frying pan and sauté the onion until soft but not browning. Remove from the heat.

Place the breadcrumbs, parsley, nuts and seasoning into a food processor until the nuts are chopped. If you prefer a smoother texture to the loaf, continue to blend until the nuts are finely chopped.

Add the onions and stock to the nut mixture and blend until firm.

Grease the base and sides of a 450-g/1-lb loaf tin. Put half the nut mixture in the base of the tin and smooth off. Cover with the remaining nut mixture and cover loosely with foil.

In the roasting oven, place the oven shelf on the bottom set of runners and bake the loaf for 30 minutes.

Remove from the oven and leave to cool for 5 minutes before turning out. Serve warm or cold.

Serves 3-4

FRUIT AND VEGETABLE KEBABS

Kebabs are often associated with barbecues, but I think cooking them in an Aga brings out the flavours of the vegetables and the sweetness of the fruit so well. Serve them with Sultana and Nut Pilaff (see below).

1 large aubergine
2 small courgettes
110g/4oz button mushrooms
3 pickling onions, peeled and halved
175g/6oz ready to eat dried apricots
2 under ripe bananas

Marinade
3 tbsp olive oil
2 tbsp cider vinegar
1 tbsp orange juice
salt and pepper

Mix all the marinade ingredients together in a non-metallic mixing bowl. Cut the aubergine and courgettes into chunks, about 2.5-cm/1-inch cubes. Add to the marinade along with the mushrooms, onions, apricots and bananas. Stir gently to coat and then leave to stand for 30 minutes.

Line a baking tray with Bake-O-Glide. Thread the vegetables onto 4 skewers and place the skewers onto the baking tray. Brush with the remaining marinade.

Hang the oven shelf on the second set of runners from the top of the roasting oven. Slide in the tray of kebabs and cook for 8-10 minutes, until cooked and slightly tinged with colour.

Serves 4

SULTANA AND NUT PILAFF

This pilaf is delicious on its own or try it with my fruit and vegetable kebabs (see above). To give a brighter jewelled effect you can use other dried fruits such as apricots and cherries.

2 tbsp vegetable oil
1 onion, peeled, halved and then sliced
2 sticks celery, chopped
225g/8oz long grain rice
600ml/1 pint vegetable stock
175g/6oz sultanas
110g/4oz pistachios
2 spring onions, finely sliced
1 tbsp chopped coriander

Heat the oil in a saucepan and sauté the onion and celery until soft but not browning. Add the rice and stir well to coat in the oil. Add the stock and bring to the boil. Cover and move to the simmering oven for 20 minutes (or 30 minutes if using brown rice).

Season with salt and pepper and then stir in the sultanas and pistachios. Cover the pan and return to the simmering oven until the rice has absorbed the liquid and the sultanas have heated through.

Stir in the coriander and garnish sprinkled with the chopped spring onions.

Serves 4

PIZZAS

Pizza seems to be ever popular with the young. I like to make my own because pizza is so quick and easy to make and you can put on any topping that you like. Traditionally pizza has a tomato base, either a thick base sauce or sliced tomatoes.

Basic Pizza Base
450g/1lb strong white flour*
1 tsp salt
2 tbsp olive oil
25g/1oz fresh yeast**
small pinch sugar
300ml/¹/₂ pint warm water

Tomato Sauce for Base Topping
2 tbsp olive oil
1 small onion, peeled and finely chopped
2 cloves garlic, peeled and crushed
400g/14oz-can chopped tomatoes
1 tbsp tomato purée
pinch sugar
salt and pepper
4 basil leaves
1 tsp chopped thyme

**if you prefer the dough can be made with 350g/12oz
wholemeal flour mixed with 100g/4oz plain white flour
**if fresh yeast isn't available stir 1 sachet easy-blend yeast
into the flour before adding any liquid*

Place the flour, salt and olive oil in a mixing bowl or the bowl of a free-standing mixer.

Place the yeast in a small basin with the pinch of sugar. Stir in a little warm water. Blend the mixture together and stand at the back of the Aga until frothing on the top, about 5 minutes.

Pour the yeast mixture into the flour and ¾ of the water. Mix the ingredients to make a dough, adding more water as needed to make a smooth but slightly sticky dough. Either knead on a floured worktop for 5 minutes or knead in the mixer for 5 minutes. The dough should be soft but manageable.

If time is available allow the dough to rise. Cover with a damp tea towel and stand on a trivet or chef's pad on the simmering plate lid. Leave for 20-30 minutes until risen. If time is short, continue to roll and shape the dough and then continue as below.

To make the tomato sauce, heat the olive oil in a saucepan. Sauté the onion and garlic until soft but not brown. Stir in the remaining ingredients and bring to the boil. Move to the simmering oven, without a lid, to allow for some evaporation. When the sauce has thickened it is ready to use. If you prefer this sauce can be made in larger quantities and frozen.

Returning to the pizza base: knock back the dough lightly and cut in half.

Brush two baking trays or pizza dishes with olive oil. Roll the dough to fit. Alternatively line the cold shelf with Bake-O-Glide and roll out the dough to a large circle or oblong. This dough mix is enough for two thick-based pizzas or three thin-based pizzas.

Spread the tomato base sauce over the pizza base, leaving a narrow border all round the edge. Put on your chosen toppings and then drizzle over a little olive oil and brush a little round the uncovered edge.

To bake: put the shelf on the third set of runners from the top of the roasting oven. Put in the pizza and bake for 15 minutes, until the top is golden brown and bubbling hot. Then move the pizza to the floor of the oven for 5 minutes to crisp the base. If you are baking two pizzas at a time put one on the shelf and one on the floor and then swap positions after 10 minutes. Serve hot from the oven.

Some Toppings

• Slices of mozzarella and goats' cheese with the tomato sauce and a few pieces of sun-dried tomatoes. Add a little fresh thyme if available.

• Spread with tomato sauce and top with a finely sliced leek that has been fried in a little olive oil. Add grated mozzarella, grated Fontina and sun-dried tomatoes.

• Spread with a thin layer of tomato sauce and add some roasted summer vegetables. Add a few black olives and a thin sprinkling of Parmesan cheese.

• Cover the base with slices of fresh tomato. Cube some feta cheese and scatter over, then some black olives. Tear over some basil leaves and drizzle over plenty of olive oil.

•Spread the base with pesto and top with some thinly sliced cooked new potatoes. Add a few halves cherry tomatoes and black olives.

PISSALADIERE

This is a slightly up-market pizza, traditionally topped with anchovies. I use feta as a substitute.

Base
250g/9oz flour
1 tsp salt
15g/1/2oz fresh yeast
150ml/1/4 pint milk
2 eggs, beaten
100g/4oz butter, softened

Topping
400g/14oz-can chopped tomatoes
2 cloves garlic, peeled
2 tbsp tomato purée
2 tbsp olive oil
1 handful fresh basil leaves
salt and pepper
pinch sugar
10 black olives, pitted
100g/4oz feta cheese

Place the flour and salt in a mixing bowl. Blend the yeast with a little warm milk and stand on the side of the Aga until frothing. Add the yeast, eggs and butter to the flour and mix to a dough, adding more milk as needed. The dough needs to be soft but not too sticky at this stage. Knead well on a lightly floured work surface until smooth and pliable. Return to the mixing bowl and cover with a damp cloth or oiled cling film. Stand either on a trivet or chef's pad on top of the simmering plate until risen and doubled in size.

Oil a large baking tray. Knock back the risen dough and roll out to fit the tin.

Place the tomatoes, garlic, tomato purée, olive oil, basil leaves, salt and pepper and a pinch of sugar in a blender or food processor and

whizz until just mixed and chopped. Spread over the dough base. Slice the feta into strips. Halve the olives lengthways. Arrange the feta strips in a lattice pattern over the tomato topping and place an olive in the middle of each diamond shape. Brush the dough edges with olive oil.

Bake on the second set of runners from the top of the roasting oven for 20 minutes, and then move to the floor of the oven for 5 minutes to crisp the base.

Serves 6-8

VEGETARIAN SHEPHERD'S PIE

Any dish that has mashed potato on top seems to be a winner with my family. You can of course vary the vegetables in this dish to suit the season, or whatever you have available.

Topping
700g/1lb 9oz potatoes, peeled and cut into chunks
150ml/¼ pint milk
75g/3oz Wensleydale cheese, crumbled

Filling
1 tbsp vegetable oil
1 onion, peeled and finely chopped
1 stick celery, chopped
1 clove garlic, peeled and crushed
1 leek, trimmed and sliced
1 carrot, peeled and sliced
400g/14oz-can mixed beans, drained
400g/14oz-can chopped tomatoes
1 tbsp fresh herbs, chopped or 1 tsp dried mixed herbs
1 tbsp tomato purée
salt and pepper

Cook the potatoes and mash them in the usual way. Add half the cheese.

For the filling heat the oil in a saucepan and cook the onion, garlic, celery, leek and carrot for about 10 minutes until softening but not browning. Stir in the bean salad, tomatoes, herbs, tomato purée and a seasoning of salt and pepper. Stir well and add a little water if the filling is dry. Simmer for 5 minutes and then spoon into an ovenproof dish.

Carefully top the vegetables with the mashed potatoes and scatter over the remaining cheese.

Hang the oven shelf on the bottom set of runners of the roasting oven, slide in the shepherds pie and bake for 15-20 minutes, until the pie is hot and golden brown on the top.

Serves 4

SAUSAGES WITH HERBY MASH AND RICH GRAVY

Sausages, mash and gravy seem very popular at the moment and so easy to do with the help of an Aga. Vegetarian sausages of various types can now be purchased from the supermarket. Choose a chunky sausage for this recipe.

8 chunky sausages
1kg/2lb 4oz potatoes, peeled
25g/1oz butter
3-4 tbsp milk
3 tbsp chopped parsley
2 tsp chopped thyme
salt and pepper

Gravy
25g/1oz butter
2 sticks celery, sliced
1 onion, peeled and finely chopped
1 small leek, finely sliced
1 clove garlic, peeled and crushed
2 bay leaves.
2 sprigs thyme
2 sprigs parsley
350ml/12oz red wine
pinch sugar
300ml/1/2 pint vegetable stock
25g/1oz butter, softened
25g/1oz flour
salt and pepper

Start the gravy first. The longer this cooks for, the richer the gravy will be. Melt the butter in a shallow, wide pan. Fry the celery, onion and leek together until softening. Add the garlic, bay leaf, thyme and parsley and cook for 1-2 minutes before adding the wine and the pinch of sugar. Bring to the boil, cover with a lid and transfer to the

simmering oven for 30 minutes.

To cook the mash, cut the peeled potatoes into even-sized chunks. Put into a roomy saucepan with about 2.5cm/1 inch of water. Season with salt. Bring to the boil on the boiling plate and boil for 1-2 minutes and then drain off the water. Replace the lid and then put the pan of potatoes in the simmering oven. Cook the potatoes for 35-45 minutes, until soft when prodded with a knife. Drain off any remaining water and return the potatoes to the hot pan. Shake well and then add the butter and the milk. Mash the potatoes until fluffy and creamy. Stir in the chopped herbs. Keep warm.

Lay the sausages on the rack inside the small roasting tin. Slide onto the second set of runners from the top of the roasting oven and cook for 8-10 minutes, until the sausages are browned and cooked through.

Remove the gravy from the simmering oven and place on the boiling plate. Add the stock and boil rapidly for 2-3 minutes. Move to the simmering plate. Mix the butter and the flour together to make a paste. Drop small pieces of the butter and flour paste into the simmering gravy and whisk. Add as much paste as needed to make a thickened and glossy gravy, as thick as you like.

Divide the mash between four warmed plates, add the sausages and pour on a little gravy. Serve the remaining gravy separately.

Serves 4

CHINESE STIR-FRY WITH GINGER

There are endless possibilities when it comes to deciding on the ingredients for a stir-fry and so there's no need to stick slavishly to the recipe. The ginger in this one adds a lovely freshness.

1 tbsp sunflower oil
3 tsp grated fresh ginger
4 spring onions, trimmed and sliced
225g/8oz can water chestnuts, drained and sliced
425g/15oz can baby corn
1 small head bok choi, shredded
110g/4oz bean sprouts
1 tbsp soy sauce
3 tsp sesame oil

Heat the wok on the boiling plate for 10 minutes. Pour the sunflower oil into the wok and swirl round. Add the ginger, spring onions, water chestnuts, corn and bok choi. Stir-fry for 2-3 minutes then add the bean sprouts. Stir to heat through. Pour on the soy sauce and the sesame oil, stir round and serve immediately.

Serves 4

TOFU STIR-FRY

Tofu is a great source of protein, however many people don't like its texture and lack of flavour. Frying the tofu gives it some colour and marinading, as I have done here, adds flavour.

285g-pack of original tofu, drained and cubed
1 tbsp light soy sauce
1 tbsp rice wine
pepper
2 tbsp vegetable oil
1 red pepper, seeded and finely shredded
1 yellow pepper, seeded and finely shredded
2.5-cm/1-inch piece ginger, finely cubed
1/2 red onion, finely shredded
1 small leek, finely shredded
125g/4oz bean sprouts

Mix together the soy sauce, rice wine and pepper and add the tofu cubes. Cover and leave to marinade for 1 hour.

Place the empty wok on the boiling plate to heat through for at least 10 minutes.

When the wok has become really hot (TAKE CARE!), pour in the oil and add the tofu. Toss and stir the tofu around in the wok until golden brown, taking care not to break up the tofu too much. Remove to a plate and keep warm.

Tip the prepared peppers, ginger, onion and leek into the wok and stir-fry well until the vegetables are beginning to cook. Then add the bean sprouts followed by the tofu and the soy mixture. Stir to heat through, 2-3 minutes, and then serve.

Serves 3

SPRING ROLLS

These beautifully crisp spring rolls are baked in the top of the roasting oven, bearing little resemblance to the greasy deep-fried take-away ones! The advantage of making your own is that you can use any vegetables you like. When I have done these in a hurry for an Aga shop demonstration I have used ready prepared supermarket stir-fry vegetable mix. Filo pastry comes in so many different sizes that I find recipes using it the most difficult to describe, so don't worry about being exact with this recipe!

100g/4oz butter
1 tbsp sesame or vegetable oil
25g/1oz rice vermicelli
1 red pepper, seeded and cut finely into strips
50g/2oz mange-tout, topped, tailed and cut into fine strips
50g/2oz carrot, peeled and cut into fine sticks
50g/2oz bamboo shoots, finely cut
2 spring onions, trimmed and finely chopped
1 tsp grated ginger
1 tbsp rice wine or sherry
1 tbsp light soy sauce
filo pastry, approx. 8 sheets

Place the butter in a basin and stand at the back of the Aga to allow the butter to melt.

Soak the vermicelli in hot water, following instructions on the packet. Drain when soft, dry and cut into 2.5-cm/1-inch lengths.

Heat a wok on the boiling plate for 10 minutes, until really hot. Pour the vegetable oil into the wok and quickly add all the vegetables and the ginger. Stir well, cook for 2-3 minutes. Add the vermicelli, rice wine and soy sauce. Stir well and then remove from the heat. Spoon the vegetables onto a plate to cool.

Line a shallow baking tray with Bake-O-Glide.

Lay the stack of filo pastry on the worktop. Brush the top sheet of filo with butter and lay another sheet on the top. Cut in half. Lay a strip of filling at one end of the filo. Roll the filo halfway down the length and then fold in the sides and then finish rolling. Lay on the baking tray and continue making the rolls until all the filling and pastry have been used.

Brush the spring rolls with any remaining melted butter. Put the shelf on the second set of runners from the top of the roasting oven. Put in the tray of spring rolls and bake for 20 minutes, until crisp and golden brown.

Serve with Dipping Sauce (see page 146).

Makes 8 large or 16 small spring rolls

TEX-MEX CHILLI BEANS

This lovely beany mixture takes very little time to make and is delicious served with corn chips or tortillas, guacamole, soured cream and shredded iceberg lettuce.

1 tbsp vegetable oil
2 cloves garlic, peeled and crushed
1 onion, peeled and chopped
2 red chillies, seeded and finely sliced
1 green pepper, seeded and finely sliced
400g/14oz-can red kidney beans
400g/14oz-can chopped tomatoes
1 tbsp tomato purée
pinch sugar
salt and pepper

Heat the oil in a shallow pan and add the garlic, onion and chillies. Fry until the onion is just turning golden. Add the green pepper, the kidney beans with juices, the tomatoes, tomato purée, sugar and a seasoning of salt and pepper. Stir well and bring to the boil. When bubbling move to the simmering oven and cook for 40-50 minutes until thickened.

Serves 4

GUACAMOLE

A perfect accompaniment for Mexican or Tex-Mex food.

2 large avocados
2-3 tbsp lime or lemon juice
2 spring onions, finely sliced
1 large tomato, skinned, seeded and diced
1 green chilli, seeded and finely sliced
salt

Halve the avocados and remove the stone. Scoop the flesh from the skins into a bowl. Mash with a fork. Work in the lime juice, this prevents the avocado darkening.

Add the remaining ingredients and stir in well. Cover with cling film until ready to use.

Serves 4

SWISS CHEESE FONDUE

This fondue is great for entertaining and at the same time gives the opportunity for using cheeses other than the usual mild Cheddar. The tradition in Switzerland is that if a man drops his bread into the fondue he must buy the next round of drinks and if a lady drops hers she must kiss all the men in the room!

1 clove garlic, cut in half
300ml/½ pint medium dry white wine
1 tsp lemon juice
400g/14oz Gruyère cheese, grated
200g/7oz Emmental cheese, grated
1 tsp cornflour
3 tbsp kirsch
pinch grated nutmeg
pinch pepper

Rub the inside of a fondue pan with the cut edge of the garlic.

Pour the wine and lemon juice into the fondue pan and heat gently. (The lemon juice is needed to allow the wine and cheese to blend well.) Allow the wine to bubble, reduce the heat and gradually add the cheese, stirring all the time, until it has all melted. Blend the kirsch with the cornflour and stir into the fondue. Allow the fondue to bubble for 2-3 minutes, until thickened. Season with the nutmeg and pepper. (Do not use salt with Swiss cheeses because they have a salted rind, the flavour of which permeates the cheese.)

Transfer the fondue pan to a lighted spirit holder on the table.

For dipping allow about 175g-225g/6-8 oz of crusty French bread per person. Cut into chunks, each piece must have a crust to skewer onto a fork without collapsing in the hot fondue. Boiled new potatoes are also delicious.

Serves 4

OMELETTES

Omelettes make an instant meal! They are perfect for adding ingredients you have to hand or you can just add a few fresh herbs. You can make an individual omelette or, just as good, larger ones to serve two. Below I give the basic method and a few suggestions for flavouring and fillings.

4-5 eggs
1 tbsp cold water
salt and pepper
15g/2oz butter

Break the eggs into a basin and whisk with a fork. Add the water and a seasoning of salt and pepper.

Heat a heavy frying pan and when hot add the butter. As the butter melts swirl it round the pan. Pour in the egg mixture and as it sets carefully draw the egg mixture from the edge to the middle.

When the omelette is set remove from the heat. Loosen the edges and carefully slide onto a plate. When half is on the plate, flip the second half over to give a folded omelette.

Flavourings

Add these to the beaten eggs before cooking:
• 1 tbsp finely chopped herbs, e.g. parsley, tarragon, chives
• 50g/2oz grated Gruyère cheese.

Fillings For Omelettes

Add these when the omelette is being folded onto a plate. The filling must be hot when it goes into the omelette.

• **Provençal**: Skin 4 tomatoes. Cut in half and remove the seeds. Chop the flesh and add a crushed clove of garlic. Season with a pinch of sugar and a pinch of *herbes de Provence*. Heat a scant tablespoon of olive oil in a saucepan and add the tomato mixture. Cook for about 5 minutes to allow the ingredients to blend and the tomato juices to dry out.

• **Lyonnaise:** Peel and slice 2 onions. Sauté in 15g/½ oz butter until soft and just browning.

• **Champignons:** Wipe and slice 100g/4oz mushrooms. Sauté in 25g/1oz butter until soft, dry and just beginning to brown.

Serves 2

SPANISH OMELETTE

The potato in this recipe can be replaced in part or entirely with peppers, mushrooms and courgettes. Make sure you use a frying pan that can be used in the ovens, either all cast iron or with a detachable handle.

4 tbsp olive oil
400g/14oz potatoes, peeled and thinly sliced
225g/8oz onions, peeled and finely chopped
6 large eggs
1 tbsp parsley, chopped
salt and pepper

Place the frying pan on the floor of the roasting oven with the olive oil in it. When hot, layer in the potatoes and onions. Cover with a lid or a plate. After about 5 minutes, transfer the pan to the simmering oven for about 30 minutes, or until the potatoes are soft.

Remove from the oven and drain the potatoes and onions from the pan and place on a plate.

Stand the pan on the simmering plate. Beat the eggs, parsley and salt and pepper together and pour into the hot pan. Immediately slide in the potato and onion mixture. Cook for 2-3 minutes until the base is setting and starting to colour. Invert the omelette onto a plate and slide back into the pan to cook the uncooked side. Cook until golden.

Serve cut into wedges with a salad.

Serves 4

FRITTATA

Frittata is the Italian version of an omelette but it has more filling and is served cut into wedges like a cake. Here are a couple of examples to get you started. Later you can experiment with whatever you have to hand. Serve hot, warm or cold, but never straight from the fridge.

FRITTATA WITH CHEESE

6 eggs
salt and pepper
100g/4oz Parmigiano-Reggiano or Gruyère cheese, grated
25g/1oz butter

Break the eggs into a bowl and beat together to mix the eggs but not to aerate too much. Season with pepper and only a little salt as the cheese will be salty.

Melt the butter in a 25.5-cm/10-inch non-stick frying pan on the simmering plate (these should be cooked more slowly than an omelette). As soon as the butter has melted and before it colours, pour in the egg mixture. Allow the mixture to set in the pan and when it is just a little runny on the top it's ready to go into the oven. Put the oven shelf on the second set of runners from the top of the roasting oven and slide in the frying pan. After a minute or two the frittata should be set but not coloured. Loosen the edges and slide onto a warmed plate.

Cut into wedges and serve.

Serves 4-6

FRITTATA WITH ONION, TOMATO AND BASIL

2 tbsp olive oil
350g/12oz onion, peeled and thinly sliced
450g/1lb tomatoes, skinned, seeded and chopped (in winter you can
use a 400g/14oz-can chopped tomatoes very well drained)
5 eggs
2 tbsp grated Parmigiano-Reggiano
salt and pepper
2 handfuls fresh basil leaves, torn into fairly small pieces
25g/1oz butter

Pour the olive oil into a frying pan and heat gently. Add the onions and stir round while heating up. If you have a lid for the pan then cover the pan, this is not essential. When the pan and onions are hot move the pan to the simmering oven and cook the onions slowly until they have collapsed and are cooked through, 20-30 minutes.

Remove the pan from the oven, remove the lid if using, and cook the onion on the simmering plate or the floor of the roasting oven, until it becomes a rich golden brown. Add the tomatoes and continue to cook until the olive oil floats to the top. Pull the onion and tomato mixture to one side, tip the pan and spoon off the excess olive oil. Spoon the vegetables into a bowl and allow to cool.

Break the eggs into a basin and beat together with salt and pepper and the grated cheese. Stir in the cooled tomato mixture and the basil leaves.

Wipe clean the frying pan, melt the butter and pour in the frittata mixture. Cook until set and finish off the top briefly at the top of the roasting oven. Serve on a plate cut into wedges.

Serves 4

VEGETABLE TEMPURA

These vegetables are cooked the Japanese way in deep oil, then served with a tasty dipping sauce. You can use a deep-fat fryer if you have one. I use my Aga wok, which works equally as well.

Please take the precaution of having a lid or cover to hand should you overheat the oil and it ignites! Take extreme care when moving the pan of hot oil when cooking is finished.

Dipping Sauce
2 tbsp grated fresh ginger
4 tbsp dry sherry
3 tbsp soy sauce

To make the dipping sauce put all the above 3 ingredients together in a basin and add 125ml/¼ pint of boiling water and stir to mix. Stand to one side.

Batter
100g/4oz plain flour
4 tbsp cornflour
salt
300ml/½ pint iced water

Place the flour, cornflour and salt in a mixing bowl. Stir. Gradually add the water to the flour, I find a balloon whisk best for making a smooth batter, whisking all the time until a smooth, thin batter has been made. Chill while preparing the vegetables.

Vegetables
225g/8oz prepared mixed vegetables, for example small
mushrooms,
carrots, aubergines, baby sweetcorn, sprigs parsley,
cauliflower florets, red peppers, courgettes
25g/1oz plain flour
light corn oil for deep frying

Prepare the vegetables as usual but keep the stalks on and cut to a reasonable size and thickness for frying. Toss the vegetables in the flour.

Fill the wok to about a third full of oil and heat. To test to see if the oil is hot enough – drop a small cube of bread into the oil, it should brown within 40 seconds.

Dip the vegetables, a few at a time, in the batter and then drop gently into the hot oil. Fry until crisp and golden brown. Remove from the pan, drain briefly on kitchen paper and serve with the dipping sauce.

Serve immediately.

Serves 4

BAKED STUFFED ONIONS

I don't know why, but some vegetables baked in the Aga have the most wonderful richness of flavour, and onions are one of them. Serve with a seasonal salad.

12 onions, all about the same size
4 tbsp olive oil
1 clove garlic, peeled and finely chopped
225g/8oz fresh spinach, washed and shredded
100g/4oz fresh breadcrumbs
2 tbsp chopped parsley
50g/2oz pine nuts
100g/4oz Lancashire cheese, crumbled
salt and pepper

Peel the onions but leave the roots intact. Bring a large pan of water to the boil and plunge in the onions, cover and simmer for 10 minutes. Drain and leave to cool until you're able to handle them. Cut their tops off and remove the middle of the onion, leaving two layers as the shell. Stand the onion shells in a shallow ovenproof dish, fitting them snugly so that they won't roll over. Chop the onion removed from the shells and sauté in 2 tbsp of olive oil. Add the garlic and fry for about about a minute, then add the spinach. Keep stirring until the spinach collapses.

Place the breadcrumbs, parsley, pine nuts and cheese in a mixing bowl. Season with salt and pepper and mix well. Stir in the onion and spinach mixture and mix well. Use this to fill the onion shells. Drizzle over the remaining olive oil.

Hang the shelf on the bottom set of runners of the roasting oven and slide in the dish of onions. Bake for 25-35 minutes, until the onions are golden and tender.

Serves 6

ROAST VEGETABLE LASAGNE

Lasagne dishes are eternally popular. They can be made in advance and cooked through when needed. I have a recipe for roast vegetable lasagne in my *Traditional Aga Party Book*. This is a variation and a little more complicated.

1kg/2lbs mixed vegetables to roast, e.g. peppers, red onions,
mushrooms, aubergines, garlic
2 tbsp olive oil
salt and pepper
400g/14oz-can chopped tomatoes
6 torn basil leaves
175g/6oz ricotta cheese
350g/12oz dried lasagne

Sauce
40g/1¹/₂ oz butter
40g/1¹/₂ oz flour
425ml/15fl oz milk
salt and pepper
50g/2oz Parmesan cheese, grated

Trim all the vegetables and prepare according to type, i.e. peppers deseeded and sliced, red onions, peeled and quartered, mushrooms halved, aubergines sliced cut into chunks, garlic peeled and left whole.

Put the vegetables on a shallow baking tray, drizzle over the olive oil and season with salt. Hang the tin on the second set of runners from the top of the roasting oven and roast for 20-25 minutes, until the vegetables are just cooked and tinged with colour. Stir in the canned tomatoes and the basil. Return the tray to the roasting oven and cook for another 10-15 minutes to give a rich, thick vegetable mixture.

Meanwhile prepare the sauce. Place the butter, flour, milk and a seasoning of salt and pepper in a saucepan. Heat on the simmering plate whisking continuously. Cook until a smooth, thickened sauce

has developed. Set aside.

Butter or oil a shallow ovenproof dish, preferably square or oblong. Ladle a small amount of sauce into the bottom of the dish and lay in a layer of lasagne sheets. Spoon over half the roast vegetable mixture and half the ricotta cheese in small spoonfuls. Pour over a thin layer of sauce. Add another layer of lasagne followed by the remaining vegetable mixture and the remaining ricotta. Top with a further layer of lasagne. Pour the remaining sauce on the top. Sprinkle over the parmesan cheese.

For a two-oven Aga hang the shelf on the bottom set of runners in the roasting oven. Put in the lasagne and cook for 30 minutes, until bubbling well and golden brown on top.

For a four-oven Aga hang the oven shelf on the second set of runners from the bottom of the baking oven. Slide in the dish of lasagne and bake for 30-40 minutes until bubbling and golden on top.

Serves 6

VEGETARIAN MEDLEY

This is a lovely combination of vegetables, lentils and fruit. You can use any type of lentil you prefer. Puy lentils tend to maintain their nutty texture more than the orange variety.

25g/1oz butter
2 carrots, peeled and sliced
1 onion, peeled and finely chopped
1 green pepper, seeded and cut into chunks
2 tomatoes, skinned and chopped
1 clove garlic, skinned and crushed
1 cooking apple, peeled, cored and chopped
100g/4oz lentils, cooked
1 tbsp raisins
2 tbsp peanuts, unsalted for preference
300g/11oz plain yogurt
25ml/1fl oz crème fraîche

Melt the butter in a large frying pan. Fry the carrots, onion, green pepper, tomatoes, garlic and cooking apple for about 15 minutes. This can be done on the simmering plate or on the floor of the roasting oven.

Add the lentils, raisins and peanuts. Stir in well and season with salt and pepper. Stir again and cook until heated through.

In a bowl, mix the yogurt and the crème fraîche. Stir into the pan mixture and gently heat through. Serve immediately.

Serves 4

STIR-FRIED BROCCOLI

This way of cooking broccoli can also be used to cook *bok choy* *(pak-choi)*, for a typical Chinese meal. For successful stir-frying make sure, before you start, that the wok is really hot and your ingredients are ready and to hand.

2 tbsp sesame seeds
450g/1lb broccoli
2 tbsp rice wine or sherry
1 tbsp soy sauce
2 tsp cornflour
2 tbsp sesame oil
6 spring onions, trimmed and sliced
1 red chilli, seeded and finely sliced
2 cloves garlic, peeled and crushed
3 tsp grated fresh ginger
salt and pepper

Heat the wok on the boiling plate. As the wok begins to heat, toss in the sesame seeds to toast them for 1-2 minutes and then turn out onto a plate. Continue to heat the empty wok.

Trim the broccoli and break into florets. Cut the stalks into similar sized pieces.

To make the rice wine mixture, mix the rice wine, soy sauce and cornflour together.

When the wok is hot pour in the oil and swirl around the wok. Add the onions, chilli, garlic and ginger and stir well for 1 minute before adding the broccoli. Stir-fry for 2-3 minutes and then add the rice wine mixture. Stir well. Scatter over the sesame seeds and salt and pepper if liked. Serve immediately.

Serves 4

SIDE DISHES AND ACCOMPANIMENTS

BUTTERED COUSCOUS

This is so easy to prepare and is good eaten hot or cold. For best results be sure to buy the best quality couscous available.

600ml/1 pint water
salt
1 tbsp olive oil
250g/9oz couscous
25g/1oz butter

Pour the water into a saucepan and bring to the boil. Add a seasoning of salt and the olive oil. Pour in the couscous, stir well, remove from the heat and cover with a lid. Leave to stand on the back of the Aga for 5 minutes. Add the butter and fork through.

Serves 4

FRUIT AND NUT COUSCOUS

The fruits and nuts give this couscous a Middle Eastern flavour. I like it served with grilled goats' cheese or simply fried haloumi cheese.

150g/6oz couscous
1 tbsp olive oil
1 onion, peeled and finely chopped
50g/2oz mixed nuts
50g/2oz sultanas
salt and pepper
parsley or coriander to garnish

Place the couscous in a roomy bowl and cover with boiling water, enough to come 1cm/½ inch above the couscous. Stand the couscous on the back of the Aga to keep warm whilst absorbing the water. Cover with a plate or cling film to keep moist. After 10 minutes fork through, the couscous should be swollen and fluffy.

Meanwhile heat the oil in a frying pan and fry the onion until golden brown and crispy. Stir in the nuts and sultanas and cook for 2-3 minutes. Stir into the couscous and garnish with parsley or coriander.

Serves 6-8

FRAGRANT COUSCOUS

Fragrant Couscous is so easy to make. It can be eaten as either a side dish or salad, or maybe try it with added chunks of feta or goats' cheese as a main course

300g/10½ oz couscous
400ml/14fl oz vegetable stock, hot
1 onion, chopped
3 tbsp olive oil
2 tsp ground cumin
2 tsp ground coriander
2 tsp mixed spice
8 cardamom pods, seeds removed and ground
2 cloves garlic, peeled and crushed
400g/14oz-can chickpeas, drained
75g/2¾ oz whole almonds, blanched
4 tbsp medium chilli sauce
2 tbsp fresh mint or parsley, chopped
salt and pepper
juice of 1 lemon

Place the couscous in a bowl and pour on the boiling hot stock. Stir well and cover with a plate. Stand at the back of the Aga.

Heat the oil in a frying pan and cook the onion until soft but not browning. Stir in the spices and the garlic and cook for 2-3 minutes, stirring all the time. Stir in the chickpeas, almonds and chilli sauce and continue to stir until all is sizzling hot.

Fluff up the couscous and add the mixture from the pan, making sure to coat the couscous well. Stir in the chopped herbs, the lemon juice and adjust the seasoning if needed.

Serves 4

STUFFED PEPPERS

This idea may seem like a cliché, but it does have a twist with a slightly Middle-Eastern note. The cooking of the peppers in the Aga brings out their sweetness.

225g/8oz long grain rice
200ml dry white wine
400ml water
salt and pepper
25g/1oz butter
1 small onion, peeled and chopped finely
100g/4oz cashew nuts
6 large ready-to-eat prunes
25g/1oz pine nuts
6 red peppers
½ tsp fresh thyme, chopped
1 tbsp parsley, chopped
1 tbsp olive oil

Wash the rice and place in a saucepan with the ½ cup of wine and the cup of water. Add a good pinch of salt and bring to the boil on the boiling plate. Cover with a lid and move to the simmering oven for 12-15 minutes. Remove from the oven and make sure all liquid remaining has drained off. Leave to cool.

Put the butter in a small saucepan and cook the onion until soft and golden, but not brown. Put to one side.

Toast the cashew nuts at the top of the roasting oven. WATCH! They only take 3-4 minutes before turning black. Allow to cool then chop roughly.

Slit the prunes and fill with the pine nuts. Cut the tops off the peppers and remove the seeds. Stand the peppers in an ovenproof dish so that they just fit in and support each other. Mix together the rice, onion, cashew nuts and chopped herbs. Use this to half fill each pepper. Lay one stuffed prune on each pepper. Fill each pepper to the top with the remaining rice filling. Replace the pepper tops. Dribble over the oil.

Hang the shelf on the bottom set of runners of the roasting oven. Slide the pepper dish in. Bake for 40-45 minutes, until the peppers are cooked but not collapsing and the filling is piping hot.

Serves 6

ROAST SWEDE

Many people roast potatoes regularly but don't often roast other root vegetables. Parsnips and carrots work well, but keep an eye on them as they burn easily because of their high sugar content. The Aga roasts these wonderful winter vegetables beautifully and it is such an easy way to cook them.

1 tbsp vegetable oil
25g/1oz butter
1 large swede, cut into medium-sized cubes
salt & pepper

Put the oil and the butter in the small roasting tin and place this on the floor of the roasting oven, until the butter has melted and the oil is hot. Toss in the swede. Hang on the top set of runners of the roasting oven for 25–35 minutes, until the swede is tender and golden-brown. The cooking time will depend upon the age of the swede. Serve with roast meat or fish.

Serves 4

ROAST WINTER ROOTS

A colourful dish, perfect for a festive occasion!

1.5kg/3lb 5oz mixed root vegetables, e.g. parsnips,
swedes, carrots,
celeriac, beetroot, Brussels sprouts
4-6 tbsp vegetable oil
2 tbsp lemon juice if roasting beetroot
12 shallots or button onions
3 or 4 sprigs thyme
salt and pepper

If using Brussels sprouts, blanch them first in boiling water for 3-5 minutes and add to the roasting tin for the last 10 minutes of cooking.

Prepare the root vegetables by peeling and cutting into fairly even-sized chunks for roasting. If cooking beetroot toss this in lemon juice to prevent the colours leaching. Bring a pan of water to the boil and plunge in the vegetables, except the beetroot, to blanch for 4-5 minutes. Drain well. Return to the pan.

Add the beetroot, if using, and the prepared shallots to the pan and pour over the oil. Turn well in the oil and then tip onto a baking tray or a roasting tin. Lay on the sprigs of rosemary and thyme. Season with salt and pepper. Hang the tin from the second set of runners from the top of the roasting oven for 45-60 minutes, until the vegetables are crisp and golden.

Serves 6 as an accompaniment

GRATIN DAUPHINOIS

A rich way to cook potatoes and make a meal of them. The cream can of course be replaced with milk, but the result will not be so rich and satisfying.

1kg/2lb 4oz potatoes, peeled
salt and pepper
4 cloves garlic, peeled and chopped
600ml/1 pint milk
200ml/7fl oz double cream
1 tsp flour

Butter a fairly shallow 2l/3½-pint shallow ovenproof dish.

Slice the potatoes fairly thinly and place in layers in the buttered dish, sprinkling the garlic and salt and pepper over each layer.

Whisk the flour into the cream and then add the milk. Pour gently over the potatoes.

Put the oven shelf on the bottom set of runners of the roasting oven. Slide in the dish of potatoes. Bake for 40-50 minutes. Towards the end of the cooking time raise the dish higher in the oven if the potatoes need browning further. The potatoes should be soft when tested with a knife.

Serves 6

MIXED VEGETABLE RING

This recipe uses Cotswold cheese, which is Double Gloucester with chives and onions mixed in. If you don't like these hybrid cheeses then choose a really tasty Cheddar or a Gruyère.

2 tbsp olive oil
50g/2oz mushrooms, wiped and sliced
1 onion, peeled and quartered
2 small courgettes, topped, tailed and sliced
175g/6oz aubergine, cut into small chunks
1 red pepper, seeded and sliced
2 tomatoes, skinned and chopped

For the ring
75g/3oz butter
200ml/7fl oz milk
100g/4oz plain flour
3 eggs, beaten
100g/4oz Cotswold cheese, grated
salt and pepper

Put all the vegetables on a roasting tray and toss in the olive oil. Hang on the second set of runners from the top of the roasting oven. Roast for 30 minutes until the vegetables are cooked but not too black and holding their shape.

For the ring: melt the butter in a saucepan, with the milk. When the butter has melted remove from the heat and add the flour. Beat thoroughly with a wooden spoon. Cool slightly and then beat in the eggs, a little at a time until they have all been added, then stir in the grated cheese.

Butter a shallow 850-ml/1½-pint ovenproof dish. Spoon the ring mixture around the outside of the buttered dish. Fill the centre with the roast vegetables. Hang the shelf on the bottom set of runners in the roasting oven. Slide in the vegetable ring and bake for 25-35 minutes, until risen and golden brown.

Serve immediately.

Serves 4

HOT AND SPICY CHICKPEAS

These can be eaten on their own or with rice. The amount of chillies and cumin you use is a matter of personal taste. I like food to have a spiciness but I also like to be able to taste the ingredients. Increase the chillies if you like more heat.

1 tbsp vegetable oil
1 onion, peeled and chopped
1 green chilli, seeded and finely chopped
2 tsp turmeric
2 tsp cumin seeds
450g/1lb tomatoes, roughly chopped
2 x 400g/14oz-can chickpeas, drained
2 tbsp chopped coriander
juice 1 lemon
salt and pepper

Heat the oil in a saucepan and sauté the onion until soft but not brown. Stir in the chilli and continue to cook until the onion begins to lightly brown. Add the turmeric and cumin seeds and keep stirring, for 2-3 minutes.

Add the tomatoes and the chickpeas and toss the mixture. Stir in the lemon juice and the coriander. Season with salt and pepper and heat through. Serve hot or cold.

Serves 4

THE PERFECT MASH

Mashed potatoes are often thought of as the perfect 'comfort food'. If that's the case then Agas are the perfect place to cook them!

New Aga owners are often sceptical about this method, but by using the simmering oven it's possible to cook them without water. In this way they keep their flavour and have a wonderful texture. Another bonus is the kitchen won't fill with steam or the pan boil dry!

The cooking time will vary according to how efficient your simmering oven is, most potatoes should cook within 40-50 minutes.

The following varieties of potato are best for mashing: King Edward, Fianna, Romano, Record, Wilja, Kerrs Pink and Maris Piper.

BASIC PERFECT MASH

675g/1½lb potatoes, peeled and cut into chunks
150ml/¼ pint milk
25g/1oz butter
salt and pepper

Put about 2.5cm/1 inch of water in a saucepan. Add the prepared potatoes and season with salt. Cover and place on the boiling plate, bring to the boil. Boil for 1 minute and then drain off the water (reserve if making gravy). Replace the cover and put into the simmering oven. Cook the potatoes for 40-50 minutes.

While the potatoes are cooking place the milk in a small jug and stand on the back of the Aga to warm through. This warming will help the potatoes to absorb the milk.

As there is no water in the pan the potatoes will not collapse, so you will need to prod then with a fork to see if they are cooked. Remove from the oven, drain off any moisture left in the pan. Replace the lid and shake the potatoes well. Pour on the warm milk and mash the potatoes until smooth. Mash in the butter and a seasoning of salt and pepper.

Serves 4

Using the 'Basic Perfect Mash' recipe, here are some ideas for flavourings.

Apple Mash

1 large cooking apple, peeled and cored
1 red-skinned apple
1 tbsp lemon juice

Cook the cooking apple with the potatoes. Grate the red-skinned apple, leaving the skin on. Toss in the lemon juice. When the potato and apple have been mashed fold in the grated apple.

Mustard Mash

Add 2 tsp of grainy mustard during the mashing of the potato.

Pesto Mash

Add a teaspoon or two during the mashing of the potato.

Italian-style Potatoes

3 cloves garlic, peeled
1 sprig rosemary
1 tbsp of extra virgin olive oil

Put the garlic and rosemary in with the potatoes and cook together. Remove the rosemary before mashing. Add the olive oil at the end.

PIZZA POTATO CAKES

Another variation on the theme of mashed potatoes. These little pizzas are a good way to use up left over mashed potato.

675g/1½ lb potatoes, peeled and cut into chunks
2 tbsp hot milk
2 tbsp basil, torn up finely
salt and pepper
2 tbsp flour
1 tbsp olive oil

Topping
1 tbsp tomato purée
175g/6oz mozzarella cheese, sliced
2 tomatoes, sliced
4 black olives, sliced

Cook the potatoes in the usual way. Mash the potatoes with the hot milk and the basil. Divide the mash into four portions and shape into flattened rounds. Coat with the flour. Heat the olive oil in a frying pan and fry the potato cakes until golden brown on both sides.

Remove from the frying pan onto a baking tray. Spread tomato purée onto each potato cake top. Add layers of tomato and mozzarella. Scatter over the olives.

'Grill' on the second set of runners from the top of the roasting oven until the cheese is melting and bubbling.

Serves 4

COLCANNON

This Irish way of cooking potatoes has become very popular in the last few years. I find this delicious with fried eggs.

450g/1lb potatoes
salt and pepper
225g/8oz cabbage or kale
3 spring onions, trimmed and finely sliced
125ml/1/4 pint milk
25g/1oz butter

Peel the potatoes and cut into even sized chunks. Place in a saucepan with 2.5cm/1 inch water and a grinding of salt. Cover with a lid and bring to the boil. Boil for 1 minute and then drain the water away. Replace the lid and put the pan in the simmering oven for 30-40 minutes until the potatoes are soft enough to mash.

Meanwhile cook the cabbage in a small amount of fast boiling water until cooked but still crisp. Drain well.

Drain any excess moisture from the potatoes and mash well with the butter and just enough milk to make a creamy mash. Fold in the onions and the cooked cabbage. Check the seasoning and serve.

Serves 4

PROVENÇAL GRATIN

This makes mashed potatoes into a quick and tasty meal.

1.1kg/2¹/₂lb potatoes, peeled and cut into chunks
150ml/¹/₄ pint milk, hot
3 onions, peeled and sliced
3 cloves garlic, peeled and crushed
2 tbsp olive oil
3 tbsp chopped thyme leaves
75g/3oz Gruyère cheese, grated
6 sun-dried tomatoes, chopped
salt and pepper
25g/1oz Parmesan cheese, grated

Cook the potatoes in the usual way and then mash with the hot milk.

Heat the olive oil in a frying pan and cook the onion and garlic over a medium heat until soft and golden brown.

To the mashed potatoes add half the onion mixture, half the thyme and all the Gruyère cheese. Season with pepper.

Place in an ovenproof dish. Top with the remaining thyme and onions, the sun-dried tomatoes and the Parmesan cheese.

Put the shelf on the third set of runners from the top of the roasting oven and bake the Provençal Gratin for 15 minutes until golden on the top and piping hot.

Serves 4

POTATO POTS

The potato pots are made a bit more special by including pine nuts. They have a great texture, always popular in my house!

675g/1½ lb potatoes, peeled and cut into chunks
75ml/2½ fl oz milk, hot
2 tsp red pesto
1 clove garlic, peeled and crushed
25g/1oz Parmesan
salt and pepper
40g/1½ oz pine nuts
225g/8oz spinach, cooked and chopped

Cook the potatoes in the usual way for mash.

Mash the potatoes with the milk and a seasoning of salt and pepper. Divide the potatoes in half. Beat the pesto into one half of the potato and the garlic and cheese into the second half.

Grease four ramekins very well with butter. Divide the pine nuts between the four ramekins. Top with the cheese mash and then a layer of the spinach. Finally top off each ramekin with the pesto mash.

Hang the oven shelf on the second set of runners from the bottom of the roasting oven. Put in the potato pots and bake for 10 minutes. Move to the floor of the roasting oven for 5 minutes. Allow to stand for 2 or 3 minutes before turning out.

Serve with tomato sauce (see page 53) or salsa (see page 69).

Serves 4

POTATO AND COURGETTE GRATIN

In the summer I am always looking for ways to use courgettes. They are not particularly popular with my children. This dish has a crispy topping and tastes delicious.

1 small clove garlic
450g/1lb potatoes
2 small courgettes
salt and pepper
300ml/¹/₂ pint single cream of milk and cream mixed
25g/1oz butter
3 tbsp Parmesan cheese, optional

Butter a shallow ovenproof dish and rub the base with the cut clove of garlic.

Peel the potatoes and slice very thinly, use a food processor if you have one. Dry the potatoes on kitchen paper. Top and tail the courgettes and slice thinly. Dry on kitchen paper.

Arrange the slices of potato in the buttered dish and add slices of the courgette amongst the potato. Season the cream with salt and pepper and then pour over the vegetables.

Cut the butter into small cubes and scatter over the top of the vegetables with the Parmesan if using. To cook put the shelf on the second set of runners from the bottom of the roasting oven. Slide in the potato dish and bake for 25-30 minutes until golden brown on the top and the potatoes are cooked.

Serves 2-3

RÖSTI

This is a traditional Swiss way of cooking potato. The rösti can be served topped with cheeses or soured cream. You can cook the potatoes with their skins on, but peel them before grating.

700g/1lb 9oz waxy potatoes, peeled
salt and pepper
50g/2oz butter
1 medium onion, peeled and finely chopped
1 tbsp parsley, finely chopped, optional

Cut the potatoes to an even size, but not too small, and place in a saucepan with a pinch of salt and 2.5cm/1 inch of water. Cover and bring to the boil. Boil for 1-2 minutes and then drain off the water. Replace the lid and put the saucepan in the simmering oven for 10-15 minutes, until the potatoes are just cooked but still firm. Drain off any moisture and allow to cool. Grate on a coarse grater into a bowl. Season the potato with salt and pepper and add the chopped parsley if using.

Melt the butter in a frying pan and sweat the onion until soft but not coloured.

Tip the potato mixture into the hot pan and stir to combine the onion. Press the potato out over the base of the hot pan. Cook for a minute or two until the base is browning. Tip onto a plate and return to the pan to cook the other side until brown. Serve hot, cut into wedges.

Serves 4

PARSNIP RÖSTI WITH MUSHROOM TOPPING

This recipe is really a cross between a rösti and a vegetable cake. I've substituted parsnips for potatoes whilst adding a little flour and breadcrumbs. Although I have added my recipe for mushroom topping, the rösti are very versatile and can be served with a variety of vegetables.

450g/1lb parsnips, peeled and grated
1 small onion, finely chopped
2 cloves garlic, peeled and crushed
2 tbsp milk
75g/3oz pine nuts
50g/2oz fresh breadcrumbs
1 tbsp chopped parsley
1 tbsp plain flour
salt and pepper
25g/1oz butter, melted

Mushrooms
500g/1lb 2oz mixed mushrooms, rinsed and wiped
1 tsp cornflour
1 tbsp soy sauce
4 tbsp dry sherry
200ml/7fl oz cream or crème fraîche
pepper
25g/1oz butter

Put the parsnips, onion, garlic and milk into a medium saucepan Place on the simmering plate and stir whilst heating. When the mixture is getting hot and drying on the bottom of the pan cover with a lid and move to the simmering plate for 15 minutes, until the parsnips are cooked. Remove from the heat and beat in the pine nuts, breadcrumbs, parsley and about 1 tablespoon of plain flour and season with salt and pepper. Put to one side and allow the mixture to cool.

Line a baking tray with Bake-O-Glide. Mould the parsnip mixture into 8 even rounds. Brush both sides with melted butter. Hang the tray on the top set of runners of the roasting oven and bake for 10 minutes. The cakes should be browning. Then move to the floor of the roasting oven for a further 5 minutes to crisp the bases.

Meanwhile, blend together the cornflour, soy sauce, sherry, cream and season with pepper in a small basin. Melt the butter in a frying pan and fry the mushrooms over a gentle heat until the juices begin to run. Pour the cornflour mixture over the mushrooms and allow to bubble, stirring all the time. Allow the sauce to thicken.

Serve the parsnip rösti on a plate with a portion of mushrooms in sauce.

Serves 4

POLENTA

Polenta is from northern Italy and is either used hot as an accompaniment for vegetable dishes with a sauce or cold and set with salads and cheeses.

225g/8oz polenta
1.2l/2 pints water
100g/4oz butter
75g/3oz Parmesan, grated
olive oil
salt and pepper

Place the polenta in a jug, this will make it easier to pour.

Place the water and salt in a saucepan and bring it to the boil. Stand the pan on the simmering plate and pour the polenta into the water in a thin stream, stirring as you do this. Stir well and continue to simmer, stirring occasionally for about 15-20 minutes. The polenta is ready when it comes cleanly from the sides of the saucepan. Just add the butter and the Parmesan, season with salt and pepper and serve.

If you wish to fry or grill the polenta spread the mixture onto a baking tray and allow to set. When it has set, cut into thin slices. Brush with a little olive oil and either place on a baking tray on the top set of runners of the roasting oven or grill in a very hot ridged pan.

Serves 4

PEPPERONATA

This is a slightly updated version of a recipe featured in my first book, *The Traditional Aga Cookery Book*. Both recipes are excellent!

6 peppers, assorted colours
4 tbsp olive oil
2 red onions, peeled and cut into eighths
1 clove garlic, skinned and crushed
450g/1lb plum tomatoes, skinned, halved and seeded
2 tbsp balsamic vinegar
10-12 black olives, pitted and halved
salt and pepper

Wash, quarter and de-seed the peppers.

Heat the oil in a large cast-iron pan on the floor of the roasting oven. Stir in the onions and cook for 5-10 minutes until soft. Add the garlic and peppers, stir occasionally and cook for 10 minutes until the peppers are softening.

Stir in the tomatoes and cook again for 5-10 minutes. Stir in the vinegar, salt and pepper and olives.

Serve hot or cold.

This will serve 8 as a starter with crusty bread
or 4-6 as an accompaniment to a main meal

PEANUT DIP WITH CRUDITÉS

This is quick and easy to make for drinks 'nibbles' or as part of a buffet.

1 tbsp sunflower oil
1 onion, peeled and finely chopped
2 garlic cloves, peeled and crushed
1 red chilli, deseeded and finely chopped
1 tsp ground cumin
6 tbsp crunchy peanut butter
125ml/4 fl oz water
1 tsp soy sauce
1 tsp lemon juice

Crudités
carrot sticks
cauliflower florets
radish slices
celery sticks

Heat the oil in a small pan and sauté the onion until soft but not browned.

Stir in the garlic and the chilli and cook for one to two minutes, and then add the cumin. Stir again, and then add the peanut butter and the water.

Blend well together and season with the soy sauce and lemon juice. Set aside to cool.

Serve a selection of vegetables cut into stick shapes or 'scoops' to eat with the dip.

Serves 6

RED ONION MARMALADE

3 tbsp olive oil
450g/1 lb red onions, peeled and finely sliced
salt and pepper
200ml/7fl oz red wine
2 tbsp balsamic vinegar
50g/2oz caster sugar

Heat the oil in a shallow, wide pan. Stir in the onions and coat with the oil. Heat through, stir and cover with a lid. Place in the simmering oven for 15 minutes.

Move to the simmering plate and stir in the remaining ingredients. Stir until the sugar has dissolved and then return to the simmering oven, without a lid, for 45-60 minutes. Remove when the mixture is sticky and thick. Cool.

Transfer to an airtight container and keep chilled. Keeps 4-5 days.

INDEX

ACKNOWLEDGMENTS

I have to thank my family for putting up with another session of recipe testing, especially my sons Dominic and Hugo who are not keen vegetarians and look forward to a Sunday roast after school food!

A huge thank you to all the enthusiastic Aga owners who have asked for this book and return many times to my Aga Cookery days. I do hope they will find some new ideas.

Of course a thank you to Jon Croft, my publisher, and his team for having faith that these books will sell!

COOK'S NOTES

COOK'S NOTES

COOK'S NOTES

COOK'S NOTES

COOK'S NOTES

Aga and Rayburn Titles
by Louise Walker

The Traditional Aga Cookery Book (£9.99)
The Traditional Aga Party Book (£9.99)
The Traditional Aga Book of Slow Cooking (£9.99)
The Traditional Aga Box Set (£29.50)
(comprising all three of the above titles)

The Traditional Aga Book of Vegetarian Cooking (£9.99)
The Traditional Aga Four Seasons Cookery Book (£9.99)
The Traditional Aga Book of Breads and Cakes (£9.99)
The Traditional Aga Box Set 2 (£29.50)
(comprising all three of the above titles)

The Classic Rayburn Cookery Book (£9.99)
The Classic Rayburn Book of Slow Cooking (£9.99)
The Classic Rayburn Box Set (£19.50)
(comprising both of the above titles)

All titles are available to order from Absolute Press.

Send cheques, made payable to Absolute Press,
or VISA/Mastercard details to Absolute Press,
Scarborough House, 29 James Street West, Bath BA1 2BT.
Phone 01225 316 013 for any further details.